BOUND TO BE FREE

BOUND
TO BE FREE

The Paradox of Freedom

GRAHAM TOMLIN

B L O O M S B U R Y
LONDON · OXFORD · NEW YORK · NEW DELHI · SYDNEY

Bloomsbury Continuum
An imprint of Bloomsbury Publishing Plc

50 Bedford Square
London
WC1B 3DP
UK

1385 Broadway
New York
NY 10018
USA

www.bloomsbury.com

BLOOMSBURY, CONTINUUM and the Diana logo are trademarks of Bloomsbury
Publishing Plc

First published 2017

British Library Cataloguing-in-Publication Data
A catalogue record for this book is available from the British Library.

Library of Congress Cataloguing-in-Publication data has been applied for.

ISBN:	TPB:	978-1-4729-3950-0
	EPDF:	978-1-4729-3949-4
	EPUB:	978-1-4729-3951-7

2 4 6 8 10 9 7 5 3 1

Typeset by Integra Software Services Pvt. Ltd.
Printed and bound in Great Britain by CPI Group (UK) Ltd, Croydon CR0 4YY

To find out more about our authors and books visit www.bloomsbury.com.
Here you will find extracts, author interviews, details of forthcoming
events and the option to sign up for our newsletters.

CONTENTS

PREFACE

On 7 January 2015, Saïd and Chérif Kouachi, two Frenchmen of Algerian extraction, burst into the offices of the French satirical magazine *Charlie Hebdo* in Paris, killing ten journalists and two policemen. Afterwards, the world reacted with a passion. One and a half million people marched in Paris, joined by world leaders who could not afford not to be seen to be there. Twitter was swimming with *#jesuischarlie*. Instinctively wanting to register my disgust at this act of barbarism, I remember starting out on my own 140 characters, but something held me back from joining in the *jesuischarlie* chorus. It certainly wasn't any sympathy for the jihadists or their cause – but did I really want to support the version of freedom exercised by the cartoonists of *Charlie Hebdo*? After all, this was a clash between two very different visions of life: secularism and Islamism, and I hold to neither.

The fiercely held vision of the *Charlie Hebdo* artists and journalists was the freedom to say, write or draw what they liked, regardless of whether it offended anyone else. It was the freedom to express their mind, even if that meant insulting or mocking others, safe behind the principle of freedom of speech that meant no-one could infringe their freedom to say what they wished. The Islamist view was the opposite: the desire to close down such blasphemous freedom as an insult to God and all that is sacred. It was the conviction that such absolute freedom was blasphemous, and that true freedom comes from submission to the law – the will and way of life laid down by Allah.

The episode made me start thinking about the nature of the freedom we prize so highly and want to protect. Soon after, I wrote a short article for *The Times* newspaper in London, outlining some of the embryonic themes of this book. The article received more feedback and comment than any other I had written in the national press, which in turn made me want to dig deeper into this theme of freedom. The result is the book you hold in your hands.

Freedom is one of the most commonly invoked ideas in contemporary life. In a cynical age, it is one of the few ideas that inspire devotion, energy, even sacrifice. Freedom is undoubtedly A Good Thing. Yet the larger question is: what kind of freedom do we want? Or better, what kind of freedom do we need? What vision of freedom gives us the best opportunity to thrive as human beings in the world?

There are of course competing visions of freedom and what it means and requires. These visions of freedom all have historical genealogies, and part of the purpose of this book is to give a brief, and hopefully accessible, intellectual history of the concept of freedom. It starts with an overview of the importance of the idea of freedom in Western culture, on both sides of the Atlantic. It continues with a brief account of some of the key architects of our contemporary ideas of freedom: John Locke, Jean-Jacques Rousseau and John Stuart Mill. It then looks at some more recent figures who offer alternative perspectives on freedom, opening out our understanding of the notion and the various ways of looking at it. The next few chapters trace the idea of freedom within Christian thought, noticing along the way a variety of views, but focusing on a particular way of understanding freedom in St Paul, St Augustine, Anselm, Thomas Aquinas and Martin Luther, showing how, although their theologies differ in a number of respects, their approaches to the idea of freedom have a kind of family resemblance and a common understanding. In the light of all this, the penultimate chapter looks at the vital concept of human rights and how useful that is as a basis for freedom in personal and social life. The concluding chapter draws the discussion together, arguing for a Christian notion of freedom that enables people to flourish better than some of the secular, libertarian models that were explored earlier in the book.

Needless to say, this book, like any other, has depended on the ideas and thoughts of many. I am always very grateful to those who discuss ideas with me beforehand, and who offer to read my books before they emerge, to help iron out mistakes, correct assumptions, spot errors and so on.

My particular thanks are due to my academic colleagues at St Mellitus College, Chris Tilling for his comments on St Paul, Donna Lazenby for pointing me to Iris Murdoch, and Stephen Backhouse for his advice on the modern history of the idea of freedom. Andrew Dilnot also gave very valuable suggestions from an economic and social perspective. I am grateful to all of them for expert and wise advice, recommendations and suggestions, and for saving me from several errors. I'm also indebted to others who read versions of the text and gave invaluable comments, or whose ideas and thoughts have helped me, including Adele Cameron, Graham Charkham, Gail Featherstone, Matt Key, Paul Marshall, Tim May, Alex Rayment, Carl Robinson, Jonathan Rust, Joseph Snelling and George White. I am also grateful to Jane Williams and Michael Lloyd for many years of friendship and collaboration, which has included several illuminating discussions relating to freedom on our regular theological podcast, Godpod.[1]

A number of others gave practical help in editing and revising the text, for which I am very grateful, including Heidi Cormell, Jennalise Kassanis and Fiona Holmer. Robin Baird-Smith and Jamie Birkett from Bloomsbury and Graham Coster have all helped make the book better than it would have been otherwise. Needless to say, remaining errors and opinions expressed are down to me, not them.

Jesus once said, 'If you continue in my word, you are truly my disciples; and you will know the truth, and the truth will make you free.' This book is brief. It does not claim to be a comprehensive account of freedom. My hope is that it helps Christian and other readers understand a little better what Jesus might have meant, and how his understanding of freedom might enable us to grow, not just in our understanding of freedom, but also in exercising and enjoying it.

Graham Tomlin
April 2017

[1] To listen to episodes of Godpod, go to https://sptc.htb.org/godpod.

1

Freedom and the Crisis of Culture

The camera pans over some barren but strangely beautiful hills, stretching into the distance. The scene cuts to a busy office, with people milling around computer screens, photocopiers and desks. Back again to the dry, quiet, rolling hills – only this time they are the backdrop to a deserted and inviting sandy beach, with curling waves stretching into the distance. A few more shots of the noisy office, then back to the beach – but now it's clear we are seeing the office through the screen of a laptop, perched on a simple wooden table in the middle of the beach. A man dressed in beach clothes and with bare feet sends a quick email, closes the laptop screen, tucks it under his arm and goes for a walk along the beach. The caption which closes the advert reads, 'Choose Freedom'.

It's only an ad for a laptop, but it tells a story which goes right to the heart of a dream that has held the Western world in thrall for several few hundred years: the dream of freedom. Given the choice between life in the city, trudging to work, battling through a typical office day, and living by the beach and doing our work with the help of a portable computer, few of us would take long to decide. It is the choice which is new – the freedom to choose.

THE LURE OF FREEDOM

Freedom is one of those 'big ideas' which define our culture. And it affects far more than just advertising. Back in 2003, President George W. Bush announced that the US and its allies had finally launched their long-expected attack on Iraq. The reasons behind it were of course complex, but in Bush's usual way he reduced them to one single theme: the defence of freedom. As he told the world that evening: 'We will defend our freedom. We will bring freedom to others and we will prevail.'

Time and time again since that notorious date, and throughout the subsequent 'war on terror', the theme sounded loud and clear. The military action to chase the Taliban out of Afghanistan was called 'Operation Enduring Freedom'. Bush's State of the Union address wound up the rhetoric of conflict yet further, and again and again the ideal which stood at centre stage was freedom:

> History has called America and our allies to action, and it is both our responsibility and our privilege to fight free-dom's fight … While the price of freedom and security is high, it is never too high … Together with friends and allies from Europe to Asia, and Africa to Latin America, we will demonstrate that the forces of terror cannot stop the momentum of freedom … Our enemies send other people's children on missions of suicide and murder. They embrace tyranny and death as a cause and a creed. We stand for a different choice, made long ago, on the day of our founding. We affirm it again today. We choose

freedom and the dignity of every life. Steadfast in our purpose, we now press on. We have known freedom's price. We have shown freedom's power. And in this great conflict, my fellow Americans, we will see freedom's victory.

Europe is no different. The European Union was set up on the basis of its famous four freedoms: freedom of movement of goods, people, services and capital across borders. Even if that has taken a hit in the light of Brexit and all that will follow it, the idea remains at the heart of the European project. Even the Brexit campaign itself was fought in the name of freedom from heteronomous control, from the stifling bureaucracy of an institution deemed to have become too overblown, too controlling and restrictive. The Trump presidential campaign in the USA was similar – promising freedom from the overbearing influence of big government, the remote Washington elite, and the interference of government into private choice. You simply cannot escape the idea of freedom. In all our political debates, the choice is never portrayed as between freedom and control, but as the question, who will offer the greatest degree of freedom?

Such appeals to freedom were powerful and evocative. America's founding had deep roots in the European Enlightenment project. The American War of Independence and the French Revolution were just two of a series of uprisings of the people against their designated and former rulers. The ideals of the new United States were the same as those proclaimed in the Enlightenment itself and, read from this distance, the language of the US Declaration of Independence reads very much as a text of its age. When the founding fathers wrote that 'We hold these truths to be self-evident, that all men are created equal, that they are endowed by their Creator with certain unalienable rights, that among these are Life, Liberty and the Pursuit of Happiness', these were classic Enlightenment sentiments, and right at the centre there it was again – the dream of freedom. Subsequently, Europeans who wanted to break away from the limitations, traditions or memories of their homelands often sought to do so by making a new life in the new continent of America. And it was no accident that the feature which welcomed them, the first thing they saw as they approached harbour in New York, was none other than the Statue of Liberty.

George W. Bush stood in a long line of US Presidents who have appealed to the same idea. It was John F. Kennedy, in his inaugural speech on 20 January 1961, who declared, in often-repeated words, 'Let every nation know, whether it wishes us well or ill, that we shall pay any price, bear any burden, meet any hardship, support any friend, oppose any foe to assure the survival and success of liberty.' Barack Obama's last speech to the United Nations at the end of his Presidency finished with this call: 'Our identities don't have to be defined in opposition to others, but rather by a belief in liberty and equality and justice and fairness.' There it is again – the dream of freedom.

It is hard to overestimate the power of this dream and the spell it has cast over the Western world during the past few centuries. Ever since the eighteenth century, people in the West have been captivated by it.

Medieval Europeans, on the other hand, had known their place. They lived in a world dominated by forces outside their control, at the whim of the seasons, disease and famine. There was not much you could do about the Black Death apart from lie low, confess your sins and hope it passed you by. Theirs was a world where natural forces were seen as expressions of the will of either God or Satan, and as a result a sense of fatalism, and an obsession with inevitable death and mortality, pervades much earlier medieval art and literature.

It was not always pessimistic fatalism, of course – underneath submission to the will of the gods very often ran a sense of trust in a God who offered salvation, and was basically on our side. The way life turned out for most people, however, was determined by where they were born, who their parents were, and the particular social and economic conditions which happened to prevail during the course of their brief lives. The idea that human beings could in any way escape from the will of God or forge their own destiny was out of the question.

Then something happened. As the unified medieval structure of church and society broke apart in the aftermath of the Reformation, as the Renaissance opened up new horizons of life, art and culture, and as science began to take a much more central role in European life, a new confidence was born, based on a dream: that humankind could actually break free from the chains which bound it. By the power of human reason, skill and ingenuity, went the dream, the forces which circumscribed and controlled human life could be mastered.

The dream persisted, and bore fruit. Technology could free us from the burden of work, as the Industrial Revolution introduced huge changes in the understanding of work and what it both entailed and produced. Medical understanding, moving beyond leeches and hot presses, could liberate us from the threat of disease and early death. New theories on the nature of society, emerging from thinkers such as Thomas Hobbes and Jean-Jacques Rousseau, as we shall see in due course, would mean a much more fluid social order – no longer would the social status of your family necessarily determine your future rank within that society. All the older institutions which gave structure and definition to life – marriage, social rank, church – were now seen as limiting and restrictive rather than liberating and necessary. Freedom from constraints was seen as the key to the future, and such freedom was sought in areas of human life even more intangible and basic than the structures of society. Economic theory suggested that the key to political and financial prosperity was minimal government and private enterprise – a free market which needed as few restraints as possible.[1]

To take just one example, many commentators suggest that geography, once one of the basic factors circumscribing and determining life and prospects, has seen its power diminished, its iron grip loosened.

THE END OF GEOGRAPHY?

The man working in his office while still on the beach was experiencing the end of geography. It didn't really matter where he was physically located – he could communicate and, in a way, be 'present' in his office even when actually

---

[1] For a classic and influential treatment of this, see Friedman, M. (1962), *Capitalism and Freedom*. Chicago, University of Chicago. See also Friedman, M. & Friedman, R. D. (1980), *Free to Choose: A Personal Statement*. New York; London, Harcourt Brace Jovanovich.

miles away by the sea. Geography, or at least distance, has become irrelevant.[2]

The roots of the retreat of geography lie in the explosion of travel. Better and faster transport promised freedom from the limitations of birth and place. Alvin Toffler's ground-breaking book *Future Shock*, first published back in 1970, highlighted the dramatic change to modes of transportation.[3] In 6000 BC, the fastest transportation available over long distances was the camel caravan, which travelled roughly at 8 mph. By 1600 BC, the horse-drawn chariot could race along at 20 mph. By the 1880s, the steam locomotive could sustain speeds at nearly 100 mph. It took only 58 years to quadruple that record, so that by 1938 planes could fly at 400 mph, and by 1958, they could travel at 800 mph. By the 1960s space capsules could travel at unimaginable speeds of up to 1,800 mph. The current human speed record is shared by the astronauts who flew NASA's Apollo 10 mission. Returning from a lap around the Moon in 1969, their capsule hit a peak of 24,790 mph. In other words, over the past 120 years, the possibilities for travel have expanded unimaginably.

The point is not just technological. The more important meaning is cultural. Executives do not think twice about a journey across the world and back in a few days just for a business meeting. With relatively few qualms we contemplate moving to a different city or country to find work, or

---

[2] To put the other side of the argument, Marshall, T. (2015), *Prisoners of Geography: Ten Maps That Tell You Everything You Need To Know About Global Politics*. London, Elliott & Thompson, is a strong defence of the ongoing relevance of geography to global politics.
[3] Toffler, A. (1970), *Future Shock*. London, Pan, p.33.

for a better standard of living – or even, should the fancy take us, moving our homes and families across continents. No longer are we destined to live out our lives within the confines of the country or region where we were born: transport has opened up the world to us, and given us freedom unimaginable even to our great-grandparents.

Travel brought us freedom from the limitations of distance. Information technology has transcended these limitations even further. First, telephones meant we no longer had to write lengthy letters which took weeks to arrive to communicate with far-distant relatives. We could speak directly, and the miles did not matter. Now, email and texts, Twitter and Facebook enable instant communication across the planet, and Skype even allows us to see the person we are speaking to, wherever they are. With my mobile and laptop I can communicate, send complex documents, and be accessible from almost anywhere to almost anywhere else. Digital internet radio means that from my desk at home I can pick up local radio stations in Leicester, Limerick, Lima or Los Angeles. The internet gives my tablet instant access to information physically located on servers anywhere in the world, in the wilds of Borneo or the centre of Birmingham. These are possibilities undreamt of even 20 years ago, and no doubt by the time this paragraph is being read, more mind-boggling potentialities will have opened up.

It is not just about technology. The nation state itself faces a new set of challenges. Once it was considered the impregnable and basic unit of political and economic geography, the fundamental division of humanity which stood out every time you opened an atlas (remember them – before Google Maps?). The internet, however, recognises no national limits. When multinational companies can operate across frontiers, often immune from local legislation, borders and boundaries no longer seem as important as they once did. Money moves across borders with the speed of a click on a trackpad. Ringing a call centre about your telephone bill in Britain will now more likely link you to a call-centre operator in Delhi or Bangalore than one in Derby or Bristol. Trade unions can complain about the resultant loss of British jobs, but the government can do nothing about it: if the telecom company chooses to move its business where it can find cheaper service, that's exactly what it will do.

No wonder a number of social commentators have commented on what they call 'the end of geography'.[4] As Zygmunt Bauman says, 'It suddenly seems clear that the divisions of continents and of the globe as a whole were the function of distances made once imposingly real thanks to the primitiveness of transport and the hardships of travel.'[5] New technologies mean it doesn't really matter so much where you happen to be in the world: if you have the means, you are free to communicate, and even be 'present' just about anywhere you like, by image, words and instant correspondence, just like our man on the beach with his laptop.

FREEDOM TO CHOOSE

Freedom from the constraints of geography is an interesting and intriguing idea, but for most people it is just one aspect of the wider significance of the idea of freedom – that freedom offers the opportunity to do what I like to do.

[4] e.g. O'Brien, R. (1992), *Global Financial Integration: The End of Geography*. London, Chatham House/Pinter.
[5] Bauman, Z. (1998), *Globalization: The Human Consequences*. Cambridge, Polity.

The liberation given by technology or by prosperity widens my options – gives me freedom to choose, freedom from location and limitation. No government, authority, religion or dogma can tell me what to do or to think; there are no limitations of space, class or morality that I have to observe. I am free to pursue whatever path of life I choose, whatever dream I may follow, as just about every Walt Disney film ever has preached. I can choose my clothes, car, job, religion, sexual behaviour, lifestyle (if I can afford it, that is) and no-one is to tell me otherwise. To offer freedom of choice is the ultimate good; to restrict it, a ticket to unpopularity. The lottery winner is promised enough cash to win freedom from the need to work, freedom from the small semi-detached house, and freedom to choose whatever lifestyle she wants, whether that means golf every day, spending half the year in Spain, or a shopping frenzy. Consumer choice remains the engine of the economy, with freeview TV offering very little apart from an almost endless choice of channels. You may not want to watch any of them, but at least you have the choice.

This vision of freedom issues in one of the most revered absolutes in our culture – the freedom to define our own identities. It is fairly common now to come across the idea that 'human nature' is simply a construct, a convenient notion invented by some people to exercise control over other people. The idea of 'human nature' was a convenient way of saying that 'my answer is right because everyone else is just like me'.

We are born with no inherent or innate qualities which define us and unite us, so the theory goes, apart from those that distinguish us as individuals. The fear is, of course, that if we are born with innate abilities or characteristics, this might somehow give legitimacy to a whole series of unacceptable differences, such as race, ethnic difference, gender or intelligence. If these were then regarded as just 'natural', all manner of inequalities might then be accepted as OK. Instead, so this theory proceeds, what we are is what we have chosen to be. Choice is exalted as the supreme good and the only force controlling human destiny. If there is an inner core, it is not something common to us all, but an individual 'self' I have to somehow discover, and the only moral imperative is to be true to that inner, individualised self.

Opposition to the notion of human nature stems from a fear that it limits human freedom. If I am determined in some way by some common 'nature' that I inherit from birth, or an idea of what human beings anywhere and everywhere are called to be, it does limit my options of what I can choose, do or become. Eliminating any prior idea of what it does or doesn't mean to be human gives me liberty (or is it licence?) to choose whatever course of action, style of life I choose, in the certainty that no-one can tell me that such choice is unworthy of humanity or 'unnatural'.

Such ideas are not unchallenged, of course.[6] Arguments for the existence of something like 'human nature' can still be found, but they don't disguise a trend in more recent thought which tries to eliminate the idea altogether.

For quite some time, people have always dreamed of escaping the shackles of their upbringing, the limitations of the accidents of their birth. It has been a staple of literary and popular fiction from Henry Fielding's *Tom Jones* through George Eliot's Hetty Sorrel to Disney's *The Little*

---

[6] A particularly strong refutation from the point of view of psychology and neuroscience is found in Pinker, S. (1998), *How the Mind Works*. London, Penguin.

Mermaid. The difference we face now is the bewildering availability of such new identities. Rather than just hoping wistfully for an escape from identities fixed at birth, we can go and buy one straight from Harvey Nichols or Gap. New Look ran an advertising campaign for a new clothes shop: 'Now your clothes can change as often as you do'. The appeal is exactly to this sense that we have no fixed long-term core, that our identities are constantly changing, and we can conform to that by purchasing a new 'look' as often as we choose. Now we no longer have to dream about who we would like to be: we can go right out and buy that look – today! New make-up, hair colour, job or even a new mobile phone cover offer new ways of construing our own identity and self-image.

THE CHALLENGE TO FREEDOM

This dream has certainly been successful. Compared even to our grandparents we in the West now enjoy unimaginable liberties and opportunities. Yet that very freedom now finds itself under threat from a number of different sources. We now see the events of 11 September 2001 as the rude awakening of the West to a new phenomenon: the rise of a fiercely puritanical strand of Islam which sought to eradicate all opposition to its own particular brand of the religion. In the West, this was interpreted as an attack on freedom – at least that's certainly how George W. Bush saw it.

Was he right? Is that what the Islamist cells who planned and executed the attacks had in mind? Is that what ISIS are gunning for – a full-frontal assault on Western liberties? To answer that requires a much more in-depth analysis of recent trends in Islam but, at the risk of oversimplifying or anticipating future discussion, a brief answer might be given straightaway.

In a sense, the answer is yes, he was right. It's not that the radicals are anti-freedom as such, but that the particular kind of freedom on offer in Western societies typified by America – freedom from the law of Allah, freedom to indulge in whatever behaviour the individual chooses – is precisely what they despise and want to destroy. The Islamist terrorists who hijacked planes, who attack European capitals, who behead journalists, aid workers and Christians object fundamentally to what they consider the unstructured moral and religious laxity of the West. It was precisely the West's cherished freedom to ignore the commands of Allah and choose different ways of life, socially, sexually, religiously, and then to spread that freedom in Muslim lands through the Israeli occupation of Palestine and a flagrant incursion into the holy sites of Islam in Saudi Arabia during the first Gulf war of 1990–1, which first inspired their hatred.

A key figure in the rise of Islamism is Sayyid Qutb, an Egyptian, born in 1906, who became involved in anti-British agitation in Egypt in the 1940s. A visit to the USA in 1949–50 provoked an increasing disgust with and hostility to what he saw as the vacuous, superficial decadence of Western culture, its overt sexual flavour and its materialist values. On his return to Egypt he joined the Muslim Brotherhood and was soon arrested for his part in an assassination attempt on President Nasser. In prison, he wrote his two most influential books, works that have inspired the Islamist movement ever since: *In the Shade of the Qu'ran*, and *Signposts on the Road*. The reasons why young people are drawn into radical Islam are complex, but the story of a devout Muslim child, feeling out of place, rejected and alienated in an encounter with brash Western secularism, and witnessing the ineffectual presence of the Christian church in Western nations,[7] is a common narrative in the background of many jihadists. Islamism is a radical rejection of the West's cherished freedoms of self-determination and self-expression.

Rigorous, radicalised Islam, which has its representatives in most major cities of the West, offers a very different vision of life – a very structured pattern which values obedience and conformity and, if countries like Iran and Afghanistan under the Taliban are anything to go by, a strict sense of hierarchy, with the word of the mullah or imam being close to law. Even if radical Islam is deemed unrepresentative and out of kilter with the mainstream of the faith, the simple meaning of the word 'Islam' is 'submission'. 'Submission' and 'freedom' – certainly freedom as it is usually interpreted in the West – are at face value mutually exclusive. At least that is clearly how Osama bin Laden and Abu Musa'b al Zarqawi saw it. It is how Abu Bakr al-Baghdadi, the leader of ISIS, sees it, and hence the radical, bitter and violent rejection of all that symbolised such freedom. As one ISIS spokesman put it: 'We will conquer your Rome, break your crosses, and enslave your women. If we do not reach that time, then our children and grandchildren will reach it, and they will sell your sons as slaves at the slave market.'

While it has made some inroads into the conversion of the West, and a number of Americans and Europeans have converted to Islam, such a vision remains unattractive to

---

[7] Qutb actually visited churches during his time in the USA, but was repelled by the way in which they seemed little different from the surrounding culture of sexualised licence. See Ruthven, M. (2002), *A Fury for God: The Islamist Attack on America*. London, Granta, pp.79–80.

most who are not brought up in Muslim nations. For most Westerners, questions remain over the status and treatment of women, the vicious internecine hostility between Sunni and Shia Muslims, and the sense of violence and extremism which lurks around the edges of the faith, as seen in recent decades in Iraq, Syria, Indonesia and India. Add to this the levels of conformity expected in Muslim dress, patterns of worship and beliefs, and the whole idea of submitting one's intellect and way of life to a revealed body of truth, and even 'ordinary' Islam still has problems in convincing the average Westerner of its merits. All the same, Islam remains a sizeable, significant and formidable presence globally, strong in Asia, Africa and parts of Eastern Europe, if not in the heartlands of the West. As such, it represents a significant alternative to the values and ethos of Western culture. Islamic theology does speak of freedom, yet it is strictly freedom within limits, limits which constitute Islamic '*hadd*' or law.[8]

Yet the challenge to the West's central value of freedom does not come just from radical Islam. One of the intriguing aspects of the world at the moment is that while globalisation spreads, local cultures thrive. Coca-Cola, McDonald's and CNN can be found all over the world, penetrating into the most obscure and isolated spots. Yet such cultural influence is only skin-deep. At the same time, we are seeing the revival of local cultures, so that we hear of 'Asianisation' in Japan, the 'Hinduisation' of India, and the celebration of indigenous culture throughout the world. The fall of the Iron Curtain in Europe, for example, led not to the establishment

[8] Gibb, H. A. R. (1953), *Islam*. Oxford, OUP, can state that 'the fundamental rule of law (in Islam) is liberty' though going on to add that due to weakness in human nature, limits need to be set to that liberty.

of universal values and a seamlessly globalised civilisation, but the re-emergence of ethnic identity as a defining characteristic of the peoples of Eastern Europe, with conflict flaring up in Croatia, Bosnia and Kosovo. The cultural logic of post-modernity, with its celebration of local diversity and individual choice, points in a totally different direction from the universal imposition of sameness, and the triumph of global culture. The 'Brexit' vote was an instance of localism raising its head again against large-scale corporate hegemony, a pattern reflected in the rise of many right-wing nationalist movements across Europe. Francis Fukuyama may have famously announced the 'end of history' in the final triumph of Western liberal democracy, yet non-Western ways are stubbornly refusing to die.[9]

The collapse of the Iron Curtain, with its strict dialectic between Communism and Capitalism, eroded the sense that there is a simple choice between two ways of life. Now there is just a plethora of diverse and dispersed options and confused powers. The result is a feeling of everything being out of our power to control. This, of course, is what is referred to as globalisation. Speaking of past generations, Anthony Giddens made the point that, contrary to George Orwell's vision in *Nineteen Eighty-Four* of a super-controlled world where every detail of life is rigidly ordered by some central power, 'The world in which we find ourselves today ... doesn't look or feel much like they predicted it would. Rather than being more and more under our control, it seems out of our control – a runaway world.'[10]

[9] Fukuyama, F. (1992), *The End of History and the Last Man*. London, Penguin.
[10] Giddens, A. (2002), *Runaway World: How Globalisation Is Reshaping Our Lives*. London, Profile Books.

Zygmunt Bauman makes exactly the same point: 'To put it in a nutshell, *no-one seems now to be in control.*'[11] There was a time, for example, when the media was carefully controlled by TV or print outlets, owned by press barons who could control the flow of information and opinion. The rise of social media has now democratised information, enabling anyone to become a media celebrity just by posting YouTube videos from their bedrooms, or blogs that are read by more people than traditional daily newspapers. Twitter and Facebook are platforms, not press agencies. By and large they do not control their content (with some exceptions), and the result is a dispersal of authority, a diffusion of voices – again, no-one is in ultimate control.

This demise of distance has led us to a new place. Geography no longer defines us. It may tell us where we came from, but it doesn't tell us where we are going. Knowing where a person was born, or where their family roots lie, may tell you a little about them, but it won't necessarily tell you where they live now, what job they do or what class they belong to, in the way that it once did. It has given us freedom to transcend the limitations of origin and the ability, in one sense to fly away from the earth-bound code which confined our ancestors to the place where they were born or grew up. It means that place matters less now than it did. Yet, on the other hand, it has bequeathed a disturbing sense of unease, that 'no-one seems in control' any more.

The problem is that freedom only takes you so far. As Erich Fromm put it, post-Enlightenment societies have

---

[11] Bauman, Z. (1998), *Globalization: The Human Consequences*. Cambridge, Polity, (italics his).

discovered freedom from the constraints of nature and tradition, but they have not yet discovered 'freedom for' – the purpose of that freedom.[12] In other words, freedom is all very well as the central value of a culture, but without further definition, in the end it only creates a void: it breaks the shackles, liberates the bonds, but it still leaves the question of how that freedom will be used, and what will fill that void. The prisoner reaches the end of his sentence, the doors of the jail swing open and he walks free, but that is precisely the moment when the questions begin. Freedom has been found, but what will he do with that freedom? Will he be able to find useful work? Will he return to crime? Will he be able to pick up family and communal responsibilities again? How will his new freedom be exercised, and how will it affect him and those he is close to?

Post-Enlightenment Western societies are in much the same place. We may have found liberty from the constraints of nature, tradition, dogma and institutions, but what will we do with that freedom? Is it just freedom to shop? Freedom to watch as many TV channels as we choose? Freedom to impose our way of life on the rest of the world? Freedom to do whatever we like? Freedom may be an ideal standing full-square at the centre of Western societies and civilisation, but it is much more complex than often thought, and not without its problems. And it's not surprising that those outside the gates, especially those without the means to participate in the global marketplace that is the consumer-driven West, don't much like the look of it and would rather go their own way, thanks very much.

---

[12] Fromm, E. (2001), *The Fear of Freedom*. London, Routledge (first published 1942).

Samuel Huntington's famous and controversial book *The Clash of Civilisations*[13] argued that future world conflicts will not be like those in the past – primarily economic, ideological, or even national – but instead they will be cultural. They will be fought between 'civilisations', understood as cultural entities characterised by common objectively definable elements such as language, history, religion or institutions. Huntington didn't confine his analysis to Islam against the West, but it features high on his list of flashpoints in the emerging world. The thesis has been heavily criticised, but it still seems to contain a nagging whiff of truth about it, especially in the rhetoric that is triggered after each terrorist atrocity in Western cities such as Madrid, London, Paris or Berlin.

Benjamin Barber thinks Huntington's analysis 'hyperbolic',[14] yet he still offers another version of the theme of a clash of world views. In his *Jihad vs. McWorld*[15] he argues that the clash is not between civilisations, but within them – between a reactionary fundamentalism (which is not just Islamic, but might equally be Christian, nationalistic or ethnic) and an 'aggressive economic and cultural globalisation' (which is not just American, either). The only way to avoid such conflict erupting into violence and disintegration, in his view, is by the advancement of worldwide civic and democratic institutions. The analyses may be different, but the binary structure of their arguments is the same – that we are experiencing a clash between two opposing visions of life, and at the heart of the battle is freedom.

[13] Huntingdon, S. P. (2002), *The Clash of Civilisations and the Remaking of World Order.* Free Press.

[14] Barber, Benjamin R, 'Democracy and Terror in the Era of Jihad vs. McWorld', in Booth, K. D., and Dunne, T., (2002), *Worlds in Collision: Terror and the Future of Global Order*, pp.245–262, Basingstoke: Palgrave Macmillan, p.248.

[15] Barber, B. R. (1996), *Jihad vs. McWorld*. New York, Ballantine.

The central idea of this book is that the long tradition of reflection and practice in Christian theology and life offers a different understanding and practice of freedom from any of the opposing forces which dominate the global scene today. It is a vision which emerged out of long reflection on the theme of freedom in Christian theology, and which frames our understanding of the individual self, of the meaning and purpose of freedom, in a very different way from the libertarian tradition so hugely influential in Western culture for the past 300 years.

Yet such a claim is itself highly controversial. For many analysts of culture and global trends, Christianity is firmly part of the problem, not the solution. Secular humanists such as Polly Toynbee, Richard Dawkins and Christopher Hitchens suggest that radical Islam is just one example of anyone who believes they are right. The real enemy of freedom and prosperity is not *al Qaeda* or ISIS, but religion in general. Whether you are Muslim, Hindu, Christian or Jewish, it makes no difference. The enemy within is anyone who believes they have the truth, because they are bound, in the end, to try to force that truth upon others. Christians no longer burn their heretics or massacre their enemies, nor do they fly planes into buildings, but given half a chance they would try to impose their views on others. To a culture that values individual freedoms so highly, Christianity's moral code and religious discipline seems alien and unwelcome.

For such critics, Christianity is just one of a range of totalitarian belief-systems that threaten or restrict personal or social freedom. With its universal claim to truth, it is seen as restricting freedom by claiming to be the final truth about the world, and insisting that everyone follow its path. In late- or post-modern pluralist culture, therefore, one of the chief arguments against Christianity is that it is inherently oppressive. The only reason Christianity dominated Western culture for so long was not because it was more true than its rivals, but because it was more powerful.

For many in our culture, freedom means emancipation from God. 'God' represents all that we have escaped from: hierarchy, male domination, an oppressive and punitive church authority. To a modern Western world that has sought to escape from monarchs who rule with divine right, dictators who stifled all difference, and totalitarian regimes that brooked no opposition, God seems just another of these oppressive rulers that needs to be overthrown.

This is arguably one of the sternest challenges faced by contemporary Christianity.[16] Is Christianity fundamentally oppressive? Is it so compromised by the abuse of power that it can no longer be trusted as a way of life for the future? Does it lead to slavish obedience and the restriction of hard-won personal freedom? Or is it in fact the key to human liberation, both at the individual and communal level? Neither this book nor any other book can provide the final answer to these questions – local Christian communities and individual Christian lives will be the final testing ground for such claims and counter-claims. A work such as this, however, can explore the potential of Christian theology to provide some answers and shape lives and communities. Does Christianity have the resources to offer something radical, liberating and satisfying? We shall see.

---

[16] Anthony Thiselton notes: 'These perspectives constitute the most serious and urgent challenge to theology, in comparison with which the old-style attacks from "common-sense" positivism appear relatively naïve.' Thiselton, A. C. (1995), *Interpreting God and the Postmodern Self: on Meaning, Manipulation and Promise*. Edinburgh, T&T Clark.

2

The Architects of Freedom

Freedom is one of the defining ideas of Westernised global culture. We cherish and protect it with our lives and the lives of our enemies. It is such a key idea that we normally think we instinctively know what it means. It may be a simple word, but it is at the same time a complex idea. This book argues that there is a fundamental difference between late modern secular views of freedom and the kind developed by some Christian thinkers over the years. We will look into a Christian theology of freedom in due course but, before we do, it is worth spending a little time trying to understand the roots of some of our current understandings of freedom in Western culture, and in particular three figures, not always appreciated in their own time, but who have shaped our ideas of freedom in profound ways.

JOHN LOCKE

The first of these was the son of a country landowner who spent his life between England and Holland, ending up as the Commissioner of Trade in London: the philosopher John Locke (1632–1704). Locke's thought has to be seen in relation to two of his immediate predecessors and contemporaries, Thomas Hobbes and René Descartes.

A generation beforehand, Thomas Hobbes (1588–1679), who had lived through the tumultuous period of the English Civil War and its aftermath in the Puritan Commonwealth and Restoration of the monarchy under Charles II, famously described the human condition, when deprived of a powerful state to keep order, as 'solitary, poor, nasty, brutish, and short'. Hobbes rejected the idea of the divine right of monarchical rule, and instead proposed a notion of natural law, representative government, and the absolute authority of the state. This authority was established by a form of social contract, which mitigated the basic human condition in which each individual was essentially at war with every other individual. Hobbes's brutally pessimistic view of human relations led him to envisage a strong role for a controlling state authority to preserve peace and prevent chaos.

Rejecting this absolutist view of the power of the state, Locke instead favoured a more democratic approach to government. Writing around the time of the bloodless Revolution of 1688, in which the Protestant William of Orange replaced the Catholic James II on the English throne, Locke supported the Revolution by an appeal to both natural law and Scriptural teaching. His *Second Treatise on Government*, published in 1689, contains the clearest description of his political thought, and consequently his view of freedom. The natural state of humanity was not the perpetual state of mutual warfare envisaged by Hobbes, but a condition in which people were in 'a state of perfect freedom to order their actions, and dispose of their possessions and persons as they think fit, within the bounds of nature, without asking leave or depending on the will of any other man'.[1] Human beings were originally created both free and equal. In this 'state of nature', however, they do not have licence to do exactly as they please, because the law of nature, ordained by God, also teaches that humans are divine property and therefore not to be used for others' pleasure. This basic natural divine law gives individuals certain 'rights', such as 'Life, Liberty and Estate', so long as our use of these rights does not infringe the similar rights of others. This state of nature, however, is always and inevitably unstable because, left to their own devices, individuals will always tend to trespass into other people's space, infringing their neighbours' natural rights. Societies and governments arise as people choose to emerge from this 'state of nature' to form social structures that avoid a state of war, which would inevitably result if there were no centralised authority to resolve disputes. This is Locke's view of the Social Contract, whereby humanity's natural state of liberty is exchanged for a degree of limitation on this freedom under central government, which means freedom in everything where the rule of law does not prescribe.

Locke views government and law, not so much as restrictive forces, as Hobbes does, but rather as providing positive boundaries, ensuring peace and social harmony. Law is essential to freedom, because without it nothing would restrain others from taking what was your own property. The purpose of law is 'not to abolish or restrain, but to preserve and enlarge freedom'.[2] Freedom is therefore the liberty to do what you want with all you possess, within

---

[1] Laslett, P. (1960), 'Locke: Two Treatises of Government' in *Cambridge Texts in the History of Political Thought*. Cambridge: CUP, p.269.
[2] Ibid., p.306.

existing laws, free from the incursion of other people into your own private space. This is a kind of freedom dependent on a certain growth into maturity, based on the assumption of reason to guide the use of freedom.

While Hobbes's pessimistic view of human nature led him to envisage a greater degree of centralised control to prevent people destroying each other, Locke's more optimistic view led him to believe that social progress was quite compatible with preserving a good degree of private freedom. Freedom was conceived as the preservation of private space in which the individual is at liberty to use and dispose of her goods, possessions and property as she sees fit; a space that is bounded by laws which, on the one hand, restrict total freedom to act, but at the same time preserve private liberties from the intrusion of others.

This was a revolution in political thinking.[3] Monarchical authority justified by divine *fiat,* rooted in the Bible or the authority of the church, was to be replaced by a contract between autonomous people, agreeing amongst themselves about the shape of the centralised authority that would govern their individual relations, and allow them space for personal freedom. It also led to new approaches to education. According to Locke, children are born under the rule of their parents until reason develops, enabling growth into a new form of freedom. Education therefore has to focus on the cultivation of rational powers as a vital source of a growing sense of independence and freedom. At the same time this new approach suggested that the individual preceded society. People did not find their meaning and place in the world through their position within a broader community;

---

[3] Locke was not alone in developing these ideas – others such as Hugo Grotius were thinking along similar lines.

instead, individual rights were prior to social obligation. Individuals did not so much find their place in the world through their role in society: instead, society was formed of pre-existent individuals, who chose to form society as a kind of secondary action, a contract voluntarily chosen, not given and received.

The other key counterpoint to Locke's thinking was the French philosopher René Descartes (1596–1650), who stands at the beginning of the tradition of modern European rationalism. Descartes is well known for his resolution to doubt everything he could until he found something of which he could be absolutely certain. This led him to his famous principle 'Cogito ergo sum' – I am thinking, therefore I exist. The thinking self became the one thing of which he could be sure, but of course that left the question of how he could build upon that realisation, to make a connection with the material world. Descartes argued that the first thing that the 'thinking self' perceives outside of itself is the notion of God, and the existence of 'certain primitive notions', or innate ideas, such as existence, number, consciousness, duration, etc.

In many ways, Locke builds on Descartes, assuming a similar rationalist approach to knowledge. However, in his 'Essay Concerning Human Understanding', Locke roundly rejects any notion of prior 'innate ideas', in favour of the empiricist view that the mind is essentially a blank piece of paper, to be written on through our experience of life. Experience is the source of all knowledge, and all our ideas come from our experience of the external world, shaped by our subsequent reflection on that experience. Just as he had argued that political freedom was a space of private liberty, where the individual was free from the demands and restrictions imposed by others, so in his view of knowledge, the individual is also free of any external pre-existing ideas or concepts separate from and prior to her own mind and experience.

The result is a new picture of a free person. This was not a person who knew their place in relation to nature and the cosmos, but someone whose freedom was found precisely in their independence of others. Charles Taylor calls it Locke's 'punctual self'.[4] Locke takes leave of any notion that we are oriented towards or attuned to any external idea of Truth or Reality. Instead, we are left to construct reality and social relations using the data which experience gives us as we make our way through life.

Locke's ideas on freedom have been hugely influential in shaping modern views of personal freedom, and even psychology, by suggesting that the self is a 'pure steering mechanism', navigating through the obstacle course of external reality.[5] They result from a turning inward, to become aware of our own activity of reflecting, and the freedom to choose objects and directions of travel, rather than there being any sense of a *right* direction of travel given from the outside. Freedom comes not through orientation to truth, goodness or anything outside the self, but instead through thinking it all out for ourselves. Freedom here is freedom from those who present themselves as masters and teachers; freedom from prior ideas that exist outside of and before the self. Freedom is individual freedom to choose and do as I please with my own resources; freedom to construct

---

[4] Taylor, C. (1989), *Sources of the Self: The Making of the Modern Identity*. Cambridge, CUP, pp.159–176.
[5] Ibid., p.174.

reality as I choose, within the bounds of a legal framework that preserves the freedom of others to do the same and prevents others from invading my personal rights.

JEAN-JACQUES ROUSSEAU

The second key figure to consider is a rather eccentric and solitary Genevan, Jean-Jacques Rousseau (1712–1778). Rousseau's most famous claim was that 'Man is born free, and everywhere is in chains',[6] or, as he put it in his discourse on education entitled *Émile:* 'God makes all things good; man meddles with them and they become evil'.[7] An earlier work, *Discourse on the Origins of Inequality*, published in 1754, outlined the foundations of his approach to the question of freedom. Rousseau is well known for his idealised description of the 'noble savage' (although that phrase never actually occurs in his works): an ideal of humanity before civilisation corrupted human nature. Like John Locke and many of their contemporaries, Rousseau was fascinated by the idea of the 'State of Nature', and thought that in their primeval state, humans were governed by two primary principles, which even preceded their capacity to reason. These were Self-Preservation and Pity – the desire not to suffer, and not to see another suffer. These were the origins of all social virtues, and kept people from harming one another. In the state of nature, humans were equal and free. In society and civilisation, they are unequal and bound.

Immediately we can see one of the contrasts with Locke. Whereas Locke saw government, law and civilisation as

---

[6] Rousseau, J.-J., (1987b), 'The Social Contract', *The Basic Political Writings*. Indianapolis: Hackett, p.141.
[7] Rousseau, J.-J. (1991), *Émile or On Education*. London, Penguin, p.11.

positive, ensuring personal liberties, Rousseau saw them as inherently oppressive. His home city, Geneva, was imbued with a blend of Calvinist pessimism about human nature, and Enlightenment confidence in culture and civilisation. For Rousseau, however, it is not the case, as Calvin and, later, Hobbes had suggested, that human beings are cruel by nature, and need civilisation to soften and control them. Instead, they are essentially and originally good, but are corrupted by the process of civilisation. Civilisation and domestication are disasters. When humans were domesti- cated, they lost their natural agility, strength and survival instincts: 'In becoming habituated to the ways of society and a slave, he becomes weak, fearful and servile ...'[8] The argument proceeds with an attack on monogamy – an invention of women to subjugate men – and particularly on property, especially the ownership of land. 'The first person who, having enclosed a plot of land, took it into his head to say "This is mine" and found people simple enough to believe him, was the true founder of civil society.'[9] This led to the inevitable comparison between what different people owned, which in turn led to inevitable envy and strife.

There are, Rousseau argues, two basic forms of inequality. One refers to the natural differences between the physical attributes of different individuals. The other is what he calls moral or political differences: distinctions established by convention and history. The first kind are normal and to

---

[8] Rousseau, J.-J., (1987b), 'The Social Contract', *The Basic Political Writings*. Indianapolis: Hackett, p.43.
[9] Ibid., p.60. Again, this marks a difference from Locke, who valued property to the extent that he saw slaves as the personal property of their owners, even proposing legislation to ensure that free men should have power and authority over their slaves.

be celebrated. The second are more problematic. Natural inequality, the physical differences between people, is exacerbated by the process of socialisation, which inevitably leads to competition and possessiveness. Society with its laws emerged when people came together to mitigate the harmful results of brutal competition and warfare, but the result was not order and a carefully preserved peace (as in Locke), but a form of tyranny. People submitted voluntarily to a supreme government which ruled according to law, protected property, and ensured defence against attack, but in that very act they became slaves, subjugated within a system of inequality of rank, wealth and power: a process which inevitably led towards despotism. This was

> the origin of society and laws, which gave new fetters to the weak and new forces to the rich, irretrievably destroyed natural liberty, established forever the law of property and of inequality, changed adroit usurpation into an irrevocable right, and for the profit of a few ambitious men henceforth subjected the entire human race to labour, servitude and misery.[10]

It would be tempting to dismiss this as hopeless nostalgia for an original state of innocence. However, if *Discourse on the Origins of Inequality* is Rousseau's analysis of the problem, his other works, including *Émile* and in particular *On the Social Contract*, propose a solution. He begins the latter with the aspiration that by shaking off the yoke of society, people can become free. It is a common mistake, however, to assume that Rousseau is simply trying to restore

[10] Rousseau, J.-J. (1987a), *The Basic Political Writings*. Indianapolis, Hackett, p.70.

humanity to some aboriginal state of simplicity without any social association. As Peter Gay puts it in his magisterial work on the Enlightenment, for Rousseau, 'the cure for modern civilisation is not return to the savage state; it is, rather, the construction of a higher civilisation.'[11] The dilemma Rousseau is trying to solve is, how to find a form of association that defends the goods and independence of each, while retaining the natural and original freedom of the human race. His answer is that 'each of us places his person and all his power under the supreme direction of the general will.'[12] By this he means not an individual ruler, but a whole community – a kind of collective being. This is his version of the social contract – a deal by which the individual surrenders her natural liberty in exchange for civil liberty, security and social order.

The resulting vision is of a system of legislation aimed at liberty and equality: 'No citizen should be so rich as to be capable of buying another citizen, and none so poor that he is forced to sell himself.'[13] Rousseau prefers small states: 'the larger the state becomes, the less liberty there is.'[14] He is opposed to representative government, as it inevitably takes power away from the people. Instead, he envisages not the kind of parliament where the people depute others to take decisions for them, but one where the people gather together to enact the 'General Will'. Individuals have to submit to this General Will in such a way that, in Rousseau's

---

[11] Gay, P. (1969), *The Enlightenment: The Science of Freedom*. New York, Norton, p.538.

[12] Rousseau, J.-J. (1987a), *The Basic Political Writings*. Indianapolis, Hackett, p.148.

[13] Rousseau, J.-J., (1987b), 'The Social Contract', *The Basic Political Writings*. Indianapolis: Hackett, p.170.

[14] Ibid., p.174. With dubious foresight, because of its small size, he predicted that Corsica would surprise the world by being the very best of states!

own paradoxical phrase, they are 'forced to be free'. If there is a sovereign, he or she can only act when the populace are assembled. Such a society can only come into being through the creation of individuals capable of the kind of moral decency and communal spirit that make such a society possible. That is why he was so interested in education, and his *Émile*, a depiction of the education of his idealised young man, is a description of the process by which the citizens of a new kind of society are to be formed.

Rousseau's 'General Will' was, in fact, a theological term current at the time which usually meant God's Will. He was intentionally trying to divert the allegiance normally given to God and the Church to 'the people' instead. He succeeded spectacularly – divine legitimacy for government was quickly replaced by popular acclaim: rulers rule at the behest not of God, but of the people.

Rousseau's writings remain immensely influential in the sphere of political philosophy, but have been especially significant in the development of the idea of freedom. Perhaps most important has been the legacy of his educational theory. The normal educational patterns of his time encouraged children to learn facts, rules and regulations, mainly from authoritative books. Instead, Rousseau argued that nature should be allowed to take its course. Children should be allowed and encouraged to study geography, for example, not by reading books about it, but by wandering in the fields, observing nature, getting lost and learning to find their way home. Émile is encouraged to read *Robinson Crusoe* as one of his primary texts on natural education, as it depicts a simple, natural way of life, devoid of the complications of civilisation, with the hero learning to use nature in its simplest forms. This was Rousseau's most influential idea – that freedom is found by throwing off customary expectations, the demands of social convention, and instead returning as far as possible to an original, pure state, which can be restored at a higher level through education.

Rousseau inspired a vision of freedom which involved a revival or retrieval of the natural state, through the processes of the General Will. This association of freedom with nature, and the idea that the natural state involves the rejection of custom and social expectations, have been powerfully influential, both on the later Romantic movement, and in more recent times. The minimalist political structure of his view of the Social Contract envisaged a form of social life and association that was as simple and as unrestrictive of individual liberty as possible.

Yet questions remain. How can the General Will be discovered? And when it is, does it not have the potential itself to become very corrosive of individual freedoms, and lead to a high degree of social control? Also, has Rousseau made a huge assumption about human freedom that ignores some more basic questions about purpose? As Isaiah Berlin once remarked, 'When Rousseau asked why it was that men who were born free were nevertheless everywhere in chains, this was like asking why it was that sheep, who were born carnivorous, nevertheless everywhere nibbled grass.'[15] In other words, is it actually true that there is any observable, original natural state in which people were free and desired freedom? And even if they did, what kind of freedom did this mean? What is the original purpose and nature of humankind – and if it is for freedom, what is that freedom to be used for?

---

[15] Berlin, I. (2004), *Liberty*. Oxford, OUP. p.51n.3 In context, Berlin makes it clear that this observation originally derives from Joseph de Maistre.

JOHN STUART MILL

The third figure we need to look at in our exploration of contemporary ideas of freedom was a Victorian Londoner, a child prodigy and later colonial administrator, who received an extraordinarily strict and isolated upbringing at the hands of his philosopher father: John Stuart Mill (1806–1873). His book *On Liberty*, published soon after his death, was an exploration of the 'nature and limits of the power that can legitimately be exercised by society over the individual.'[16] Like Locke, Mill struggled with the relationship between individual liberty and authority, assuming there was a fundamental opposition between them. He wanted to establish the limit to which collective opinion could interfere with individual independence: freedom from what he called the 'tyranny of the majority' – the very thing that Rousseau's idea of the 'General Will' seemed to imply.

Mill argues that the only valid reason for interfering with the liberty of action of any particular person is to protect them from physical harm. It is never justifiable to interfere with another person's freedom to ensure their happiness, wisdom or well-being, because that is to determine what that person's well-being is. Mill, as a creature of his age, did not argue that liberty was essential to all human societies. Despotism was appropriate in less developed or enlightened societies, where individuals had not progressed enough to the stage where they could use their freedom wisely. Freedom is defined, first, as liberty of conscience, thought, feeling and opinion; second, as 'liberty of tastes and pursuits … doing as we like … without impediment from our fellow

---

[16] Mill, J. S. (1998), *On Liberty and Other Essays*. Oxford, OUP, p.5.

creatures, so long as what we do does not harm them', and, third, the 'freedom to unite for any purpose not involving harm to others'.[17]

Mill is one of the great champions of nonconformity in thought and action. Even if just one person held a particular opinion while everyone else in the world held the opposite, there would be no justification in silencing that one voice. Periods of history when the yoke of authority has been broken have tended to lead to periods of human exploration and innovation. Discussion and intellectual exploration are everything: once an idea becomes general opinion, it tends to get dull, stop progressing, and begins to decline. For Mill, one of the main ingredients of social progress is freedom from the traditions and customs imposed by others, which restricts the cultivation of individuality, which in turn 'is one of the leading essentials of well-being'.[18] Individual liberty is vital, not just for the sake of the individual, but for the sake of human progress. Without it there will be no originality or genius, no new discoveries or innovation. Civilisation cannot advance without a degree of individual freedom which encourages spontaneous expression, the development of new thoughts and ideas unconstrained by the patterns of the past.

There are therefore strict limits to the authority of society over the individual. Mill holds to a distinction between matters that only involve the individual, and matters which concern society as a whole. Where only the individual is concerned, society has no right to intervene – it can restrict personal liberty only where society itself is threatened or

[17] Ibid., p.17.
[18] Ibid., p.63.

affected by the threat of harm towards others. Society can express disapproval of individual action purely by advice, instruction, persuasion or avoidance, never by legislating against personal choice, so long as that personal choice does not harm others. This is Mill's passionate defence of personal freedom, which is ultimately described in this way: 'Liberty consists in doing what one desires'.[19]

On Liberty is full of the fear of Victorian conformity – the individualist's reaction to a stifling society with a high degree of social control. It is very much a book of its time, in assuming the cultural superiority of the modern age, and, it must be said, in lacking any awareness of the contextual nature of all thinking. It breathes an elitism that looks down on the mediocrity of what it calls 'average men'. As such, in more recent times it has been subjected to rigorous critique. For example, Mill's idea of a sphere of self-regarding actions that affect no one else – does that really exist? Are there *any* actions we take that don't affect others in one sense or another – especially in an age of social media, where almost every action seems to be potentially public, affecting others for better or worse? Similarly, what is meant by the principle of 'harm'? What if one individual finds the opinions of others an offence to their feelings – is that harmful to their own interests? Are his key ideas, at the end of the day, rather vague generalities which don't get us very far in practice? He offers a stirring challenge to a suffocating and repressive social order, which may have been relevant to Victorian England, but perhaps doesn't offer much to a society where, as Isaiah Berlin points out, people 'are terrified of disintegration and too little direction … alarmed by the prospect of

[19] Ibid., p.107.

too much freedom which leaves them lost in the vast friendless vacuum, a desert without paths or landmarks or goals'.[20]

In addition, there is a good deal of evidence that individualism and new ideas emerge from highly disciplined and structured communities, such as medieval monasteries, which nurtured figures like Duns Scotus or Thomas Aquinas, rather than just in modern liberal societies with their high degree of individual freedom. Mill's is a comparatively modern idea, and its absence does not seem to have restricted innovation of thought and enquiry before the nineteenth century! Having said all that, his is a classic and passionate statement of individual liberty and, like the thought of Locke and Rousseau, has been hugely influential on subsequent political and cultural understandings of freedom.

FREEDOM AS WE KNOW IT

These three thinkers have had an enormous influence on our contemporary assumptions about freedom. Locke's idea of the state as the guardian of personal space and freedom, Rousseau's idea of civilisation as corrupting the purity of original nature and Mill's vision of the individual's freedom from the tyranny of social convention have each shaped our instinctive views of freedom more often than we realise.

While the idea that there are limits to state and church power can be traced back long before John Locke, and was, for example, one of the key insights of the Reformation, Locke was one of the first to assert the freedom of the individual from inherited or innate ideas, and the individual's right to an inviolable space in which to act as he chose. The

---

[20] Berlin, I. (2002a), 'John Stuart Mill and the Ends of Life', *Liberty*: 218–51. Oxford: OUP, p.243.

idea that I have the right to use my own possessions and property in the way I choose, as long as I am mindful of the rights of others, as established by some kind of natural law, is one that can be traced back to his thinking at the dawn of the modern age.

Similarly, the common idea that freedom is found by throwing off the shackles of custom and civilisation, and returning to some form of natural state, free of the constraints and complications of society, is one we owe to the thinking of Jean-Jacques Rousseau, even if his own thought on social relations and the General Will is a little more complex than this. We like things to be 'natural' and uncomplicated by human interference, whether breakfast cereal, food ingredients or hair colour, and that we tend to think of something being 'natural' as a good thing is because we tend to believe Rousseau rather than Hobbes.

The notion of the sacrosanct nature of individual freedom of expression, that I have an absolute right and responsibility to be myself, to think for myself, and not to conform to the expectations and demands of others, owes a great deal to a number of thinkers who propounded this approach to liberty, climaxing in Mill's passionate defence of individual liberties in the nineteenth century. The classical liberal tradition, which preserves individual liberty as a central tenet, is rooted in the prolonged development through history of basic Christian anthropology, a story told admirably by Larry Siedentop,[21] yet this particular form of it – the absolute right of the individual to self-expression and freedom of opinion – owes a great deal to Mill's influential work. All

---

[21] Siedentop, L. (2014), *Inventing the Individual: The Origins of Western Liberalism.* London, Allen Lane.

these thinkers are key architects of freedom as we understand it in the modern Western world.

One way of pulling all this together is the analysis of freedom in a couple of seminal texts on the idea of freedom in the twentieth century. The first is Isaiah Berlin's 'Two Concepts of Liberty'.[22] Starting by observing the complexity of the concept of freedom (he claims there are at least 200 senses in which the word is used), Berlin makes a distinction between negative and positive freedom. *Negative* freedom means a state of not being constrained by others; being left to follow my own path, without interference from anyone else. I am free to the extent that no one else tries to stop me doing what I want to do. The larger the space of my own autonomy, free from interference by others, the greater my freedom. This is the kind of freedom envisaged by both Locke and Mill, along with others such as Hobbes and Jeremy Bentham. They disagree on the extent of this freedom and its boundaries, but are all concerned to define freedom negatively, in the sense of a lack of interference by others who might stop me doing what I choose. This is what Berlin calls 'liberty from':[23] the absence of encroachment of others on my own private personal space.

On the other hand, *positive* freedom concerns the extent to which I am my own master. It refers to the question of who governs me, who directs my actions and my life. Do I do it myself, or am I controlled by someone else – parents, priests, or policemen? To what extent am I master of my own fate? This is 'liberty to': a sense of what I do with my newly found freedom, and who I choose, voluntarily, to

[22] Berlin, I. (2002b), 'Two Concepts of Liberty' in H. Hardy (Ed.), *Liberty*, New York: OUP, pp.166–217.
[23] Ibid., p.174.

submit to. This kind of 'positive freedom', Berlin points out, can be abused, in that various authorities can present themselves as offering a path to betterment, if I only pledge true obedience to them – people who claim to know what is good for me better than I know myself, whether that be a political party, a church, or a mentor.

A similar analysis was made during the Second World War by the German social psychologist Erich Fromm.[24] In response to the frightening rise of Nazism in Europe, he developed a psychological account of the growth of European society towards freedom. The medieval world was for him characterised by a lack of freedom, with people chained to their role within the social order. As such, the 'individual' did not yet exist. It only began to emerge with the break-down of the feudal state and the emergence of Renaissance capitalism. The new economic structures of the emerging world freed the individual from economic and social ties, but also took away the security those bonds gave him – leaving him free, but also alone and threatened. The new capitalists of the Renaissance could enjoy this 'positive freedom'. The middle classes, however, left out of this financial bonanza, experienced isolation, insignificance and resentment, which found an answer in the Reformation's offer of certainty and significance through the power of faith. This new independence gave 'freedom from', but did not establish 'freedom to'.

In the modern world, according to Fromm, the more independent and self-reliant we become, the more isolated we also feel. Capitalism left the individual to stand on his own. Protestantism left him to face God on his own. Hobbes left the individual to the mercy of the all-powerful state. The

---

[24] Fromm, E. (2001), *The Fear of Freedom*. London, Routledge.

result was isolation and powerlessness, a vision articulated dramatically in the work of figures such as Kierkegaard, Nietzsche and Kafka. We are simply not yet able to cope with 'freedom from'. And so a citizen of this modern world flees to authoritarian leaders and structures (at this point, you can clearly see the shadow of Nazism), because he or she cannot cope with the solitude of freedom from the old bonds: 'he finds new and fragile security at the expense of sacrificing the integrity of his individual self. He chooses to lose his self since he cannot bear to be alone. Thus freedom – as freedom from – leads into new bondage'.[25]

The answer, Fromm suggests, that is found in self-realisation: a kind of spontaneity of the kind found in children and artists. This positive freedom is not yet realised, but remains an ideal. In fact, society exists for the purpose of enabling this kind of freedom to emerge.

Both Berlin and Fromm clearly define 'freedom from' – this sense that the last few centuries have seen liberation from constraints that felt like shackles. And yet at the same time, while they both point to a new kind of 'freedom for', neither seems able to identify what it actually looks like. Berlin is afraid it will lead to new forms of servitude and oppression. Fromm thinks the human race is not yet ready to live in its new-found freedom, and still turns to authoritarian control out of fear of the emptiness of the New World into which we have arrived.

THE USES OF FREEDOM

Locke, Rousseau and Mill are all concerned, in different ways, to safeguard a space for individual liberty. Yet when

---

[25] Ibid., p.221.

they come to make positive proposals as to how that freedom is actually to be used, rather than just protected, the picture gets less clear.

Each of these three thinkers is an architect of the kind of freedom we take for granted in modern Western societies. Yet striving for freedom to pursue our own good, or freedom from the demands that others place upon us, led inevitably to the question of what guarantees that freedom, and in each case this led to the growing power of the state.

Locke may have been reacting to Hobbes's heavy-handed and controlling state, and yet for him the only thing that guarantees individual freedom is the state itself, which then becomes the guarantor of freedom and rights. His 'punctual self' is left alone in the universe to construct its own reality, and there is always the lurking fear that the state simply replaces God as the moulder and shaper of character. Locke's idealism assumes that the mind starts with a blank slate, not influenced by innate ideas – a notion that sounds innocent enough, yet, applied to his political philosophy, could have more ambivalent, darker overtones. As Terry Eagleton put it: 'John Locke's doctrine that the mind is originally a *tabula rasa* could be used to banish the spectre of original sin, thus countering a view of men and women as innately depraved with a sanguine trust in the power of social engineering to mould them into virtue'.[26]

Rousseau had a horror of civilisation and its effects, and yet his idea of the General Will opens the door to a high degree of social control, where the individual has

---

[26] Eagleton, T. (2014), *Culture and the Death of God*, p.13.

the prospect of being 'forced to be free'. Rousseau does not have the confidence in the progress of civilisation that Locke does, and nostalgically appeals to a return to nature, and a minimal state, to establish freedom. However, in practice his concept of the 'General Will' is notoriously hard to pin down, and how it might be discovered is difficult to imagine. As Isaiah Berlin pointed out, it is very vulnerable to being taken over by a small group who are quite happy to assert what it is, against which the individual has no comeback whatsoever. Rousseau's claim that in such a society individuals are 'forced to be free' has a slightly chilling tone to it, and raises the dark spectre of totalitarian control.

Mill fights jealously for the space of personal freedom, but does it really exist? Mill avoids eliding this domination of the individual into the 'tyranny of the majority' through his fervent defence of individual freedom to think and act and speak for oneself. However, when analysed closely, this realm of purely personal action which affects no one else disappears into nothing, like sand slipping through the fingers, offering little help to those feeling atomised and directionless in the early twenty-first century. If there really are very few actions that don't affect others, all we have left is a state that polices anything which might *seem* to harm others, which turns out to be quite a lot of things!

The problem is that freedom defined as the ability to choose one's own path, within the limits placed on such freedom by other people, is deeply problematic. The freedom that exists within my own personal space has no particular shape, no content other than that which I choose to give it. Terry Eagleton again: 'The freedom which modern civilisation prizes as its spiritual essence is also a kind of vacancy at its heart'.[27] As soon as you try to build something and begin to collide with the demands of others, like bumper cars at a fair, it feels like an inhibition of that freedom.

In this formulation, other people are not a gift but a threat to my freedom. Limits feel like obstacles. I need state power to police the boundary of my jealously guarded freedoms, but that state power itself becomes a menace, and something I need to watch carefully lest it begin to encroach upon my freedom. Pushed to its logical conclusion, the freedom envisaged by all three of these thinkers, Locke, Mill and Rousseau, can only be found in solitude.

It is also ironic that the emphasis on 'individual freedom' that comes from this trio of philosophers has led to the increase and influence of the state in everyday life. Libertarians constantly bemoan 'big government', but in a world where no idea of the common good can be imposed, assumed or expected, eventually the only way to prevent one individual's freedom from impinging on another's turns out to be a forest of bureaucracy.

Each one of these thinkers was fascinated by the question of the 'state of nature': the original condition of humanity. Whereas traditional Christian theology refused to countenance any way back to Eden, past the 'turning and flaming sword' which blocked the way back to the tree of life (Genesis 3.24), each of these three philosophers thought he had found a way round the back. For Locke, the detour led through the idea of individual rights, guaranteed by natural law, freed once and for all from innate ideas. For Rousseau, the path meandered through a recovery of the natural, as simple and uncomplicated a social life as possible while

---

[27] Eagleton, T. (2005a), *Holy Terror*. Oxford, OUP, p.75.

remaining compatible with social order. For Mill it was the guarding of precious space for individual choice and expression. The question remains whether there is such a way back to Eden. Or is the road blocked with much bigger obstacles than any of them thought? Are we really as free as we think we are?

3

The Illusion of Freedom

The quest for freedom, whether the freedom of nations striving for independence from imperial control, or the individual from social conformity, was shaped and moulded through the seventeenth, eighteenth and nineteenth centuries by the kind of thinkers we considered in the last chapter. The latter part of this period saw the great movements of emancipation of nations, as different peoples around the world sought freedom from imperial control. The American and French Revolutions of 1776 and 1789 were perhaps the most dramatic, followed in turn by a whole series of revolutions in the nineteenth and twentieth centuries as, one by one, peoples broke away from former rulers to form their own new nation states.

In these centuries, the narrative of emancipation grew beyond nations to groups of people: Protestants, Catholics, slaves, blacks, Jews, women, LBGTI, and many more. Two world wars saw the threat of totalitarian control resisted in far-ranging battles for freedom from tyranny. In the twentieth century, walls were put up in Europe to control and divide, and then broken down again to usher in what was hoped would be new eras of prosperity and liberty. As a result, the twentieth century could be seen as the century when freedom made its greatest strides. Freedom and the related ideas of democracy and human rights seemed to make progress across the world, leading Francis Fukuyama to make his famous declaration of the 'end of history', in that civilisation had supposedly reached its culmination in liberal democracy and freedom, the fruit of the ideas sketched out by the luminaries we considered in the last chapter.

Yet despite all this, there is still a nagging doubt that remains at the heart of this dream of freedom. And the doubt is that we are not actually as free as we think we are. This chapter considers three very different twentieth-century thinkers who, in different ways, all question the notion of an inevitable progression towards freedom.

FREEDOM AND POWER

One of the twentieth century's most influential thinkers was the French philosopher Michel Foucault. His primary work consisted of a series of histories, or narratives, not so much of historical periods, as of concepts such as sexuality, prisons, insanity and mental illness. He was interested in history less as a way of discovering 'what really happened', more because it can help us to examine what we think to be evidently true, and uncover all kinds of hidden dynamics that make us think the way we do. Foucault does not believe we can have objective facts which then need interpretation; all history does is to examine the interpretations. He has no desire to uncover the truth about things, but rather hopes to display the arbitrary and contingent nature of 'discourses'. As a result, he is sceptical about the notion that Western societies are progressing forwards in an inevitable march to the sunny uplands of freedom.

Foucault's histories are intended to uncover a lack of cohesion in history. They show how there is no guiding intention, no underlying reality to be discovered, and, more pertinently, how there is no one in control. The goal is not to uncover some secret purpose or intention in history, but simply to try to help us see how power operates in specific institutions of society, such as in prisons and penitentiaries, madhouses, psychiatric units and so on. It is a question of identifying not so much who has power and how they use it, but how power works in practice. If history has no inner meaning, and is just a constant struggle between forces, he wants to show how those forces interact. So, for example, in his analysis of madness, he writes of the creation of the lunatic asylum in Paris in the seventeenth century. This, he claims to demonstrate, was a means of isolating an under-class of people, ending unsightly and socially inconvenient unemployment and begging, by placing them in institutions which kept them away from the rest of society. In his analysis of the penal system, nineteenth-century prisons, rather than being a socially progressive means of punishing vice, or isolating criminals from society, effectively became a way of organising the criminal class, and keeping them criminal, so that they were able to run the black market, without which the whole series of social functions would have fallen apart.

For Foucault, truth is intimately connected with power. Power does not so much repress an underlying reality, as produce new versions of reality. Truth produces power, and power produces truth. Foucault encourages his readers to discover the power dimensions at work in any particular context. In any social interaction, whether a business, a university, a church, a marriage or friendship, there are power dynamics at work. Each of these will have a discourse as to how truth operates within it, but Foucault is sceptical about those discourses – they are usually arbitrary, and are used to justify a set of power relations.

Likewise, Foucault resists the idea of a gradual process of enlightenment, whereby society is thought to progress towards greater degrees of understanding and freedom. In his early years, he was an avowed Marxist, but in his later career he gradually moved away from that position. Classical Marxism suggested that power was concentrated in the hands of the owners of the means of production, and needed to be wrested from them into the hands of the proletariat, so that the workers could own the means of production. Foucault came to believe that it was not quite so simple – power could never be concentrated in any one place, either with the bourgeoisie, or the proletariat. In fact, revolutions don't tend to improve things – they are simply the replacement of one set of arbitrary and contingent values by another. Trying to grasp power is like trying to grab water out of a bowl with your hands: as soon as you try it slips through your fingers.

In any institution, it seemed to Foucault, power never works in a simplistic top-down fashion, but rather operates in a dispersed network. Power relations are present in all human relationships. They are endemic and inevitable in human society. They cannot be abandoned, and must not be ignored. They work through unseen mechanisms, never orchestrated by anyone in particular. It is not so much that power is the deliberate repression of one by another – that would imply that power can be concentrated in one place. Instead, these relations of power are a web in which we are caught. Only local resistance is possible; a kind of 'pessimistic activism'.

Foucault has been described by John Rajchman as 'the great sceptic of our times',[1] and by Alan Sheridan as 'a slayer of dragons, a breaker of systems'.[2] Foucault's vision of society is therefore one in which freedom is very circumscribed. We may think we are free, but in fact we are caught in a vast interaction of power relations, in which we have very little liberty to move.

His is a voice that raises a significant question mark over the simple narrative that suggests that humanity is progressing from a benighted past of slavery towards a state of pure liberty. At least he raises the issue of ideology: is the march to freedom the real story? Or is entrapment in systems of power and control inevitable in human society and culture? If so, maybe all we can do is try to be aware of our lack of freedom, and the ways in which power operates around us, and so try to create some small space for personal freedom.

FREEDOM AND THE ROOTLESS SELF

One of the most penetrating and authoritative writers on the notion of identity in recent years is the Canadian philosopher Charles Taylor. Towards the end of his magnificent (and very long) book *Sources of the Self*, he writes:

> The kind of study I have embarked on here can be a work, we might say, of liberation. The intuition which inspired it ... is simply that we tend in our culture to

---

[1] Rajchman, J. (1985), *Michel Foucault: The Freedom of Philosophy*. New York; Guildford, Columbia University Press, p.2.
[2] Sheridan, A. (1980), *Michel Foucault: The Will to Truth*. London, Routledge, p.225.

stifle the spirit … We have read so many goods out of our official story, we have buried their powers so deep beneath layers of philosophical rationale, that they are in danger of stifling. Or rather, since they are our goods, human goods, *we* are stifling.[3]

Taylor's account of the self is a kind of narrative of freedom, but one very different from those we have been considering so far. It is worth examining closely, as a way of exploring this uncomfortable sense that the promise of freedom may not be all that it seems.

Taylor charts a development that begins with the 'engaged self' of Plato and others in the ancient world. This was a self which was rooted in the wider cosmic order and had a sense of its own place within an already predetermined structure. The Platonic view of the world saw the visible, phenomenal world as an imperfect copy of ideal Forms, existing on an invisible metaphysical plane. What we see and experience is therefore grounded in a wider, fixed natural order to which it always has reference. The self therefore existed with reference to that fixed order, and its task was to adapt and attune itself to it – an idea particularly developed in Stoicism. The self therefore naturally turns outwards to find moral power and meaning, rather than finding it in its own interior life.

Taylor then moves on to a brief discussion of Augustine's 'inwardness', which, although a turn inwards into introspection, is an examination of the soul in relation to God. In other words, while this does represent something of a shift from the Platonic view of the self, it is still rooted in a wider

[3] Taylor, C. (1989), *Sources of the Self: The Making of the Modern Identity*. Cambridge, CUP, p.520.

sense of given order, with the soul, aided by grace, learning to grow in love and being loved. Augustine after all, was heavily influenced by his early dalliance with Platonism, and his thought always retained something of a Platonic cast of mind, with its orientation towards God as the sole source of all that was beautiful, good and true.

Taylor then explores Descartes's view of the 'self', which we touched on in the last chapter. Descartes rejected any sense of an outward order, including Plato's theory of Forms or Ideas. As in in Augustine, the self turns inwards, to its own thinking processes, in order to find moral orientation and direction, though this time, unlike Augustine, without any assumed rootedness in a divine order outside itself. With no order of natural ideas to turn to, the self steps outside both the natural order of things, and even the embodied self, into the world of the mind. The result is a disengagement of the self from any wider order or structure of being outside its own consciousness, a 'disengagement from world and body and the assumption of an instrumental stance towards them'.[4] Although, as with Augustine, this is a turn inwards, it is a very different kind of turn. When Augustine looks within, he finds God, who made humanity in his own image. Descartes's knowledge, on the other hand, is 'unconditional and self-generated'.[5] God still appears in Descartes's scheme, but rather than being the object of discovery in the process of introspection, he is merely the secondary inference arising out of a prior self-awareness. As Taylor puts it, in turning within, whereas Augustine discovers God, Descartes discovers himself.

[4] Ibid., p.155.
[5] Ibid., p.157.

The discussion proceeds to John Locke, and the idea (as we have already seen) of what Taylor calls the 'punctual self'. Descartes had denied Plato's notion of pre-existent Forms or Ideas, but still maintained that there were some basic, innate ideas that could be perceived by the mind, such as the idea of God. As we saw in the last chapter, Locke went further than Descartes in denying any innate ideas altogether, preferring to think that our conceptions of the world were self-generated, written on the blank slates of our minds through experience and reflection. This is an even more radical disengagement from anything external. There is no exterior truth or order towards which human beings are oriented. The self disengages also from its own unreflective processes of thought or desire, becoming capable of reflection on the self as an object quite distinct from the wider world, and even its own thought processes. As Taylor puts it, 'radical disengagement opens the prospect of self re-making'.[6] He calls this the 'punctual self' because it distances itself as a distinct point, remote from anything which might impact upon it. This is a self distinguished from other selves, from any external order which might place it in a wider given context, and even from its own existence.

And here we come to the key point: Taylor argues, therefore, that the very notion of the 'self' is a modern one. 'We have come to think that we "have" selves as we have heads. But the very idea that we have or are "a self", that human agency is essentially defined as "the self", is a linguistic reflection of our modern understanding and the radical reflexivity it involves ... But it was not always so.'[7] This is

---

[6] Ibid., p.171.
[7] Ibid., p.177.

what he calls the 'inward turn', which is for Taylor the key to understanding modernity.

The result is a disenchantment with the world, with no wider sacred structure into which human life naturally fits. It has led to a more profoundly individualistic culture, with our 'punctual selves' at some distance from one another. It has eroded any sense of a higher purpose and passionate engagement, rather leaving behind a more self-absorbed, solipsistic focus on individual lives, often leading to reluctance or unwillingness to engage in corporate life, politics or government. It also leads to the dominance of what Taylor calls 'instrumental reason', which seeks maximum efficiency and the maximisation of wealth and income, because there are no larger or more compelling purposes to aim for. In the absence of any grounding in the order of things or the will of God, social arrangements can be redesigned with the goal of the well-being and prosperity of the individual in mind. Other people are no longer necessarily given to us by someone or something outside ourselves, demanding our respect or even reverence. Instead they become instruments to achieve broader goals in some Machiavellian way – or even obstacles in the way of attaining my own self-fulfilment.

These trends can also lead to the dominance of technology – the thinness of modern life where tasks are achieved at the press of a button, rather than requiring the combined work of a whole community, or where communication is reduced to a 140-character tweet, rather than an in-depth conversation.[8] The dominance of instrumental reason, the widely held belief in a market imperative to strive for

---

[8] These ideas are developed particularly in Taylor, C. (1991), *The Ethics of Authenticity*. Cambridge, Mass., Harvard University Press.

maximum efficiency and profit, means that our choices are in fact restricted, not necessarily enlarged. For example, it becomes almost impossible to address the urgent need for action on global climate change, to turn the tide on the pollution of the earth's oceans with plastic waste, or address the prevalence of conflict and poverty, driving mass migrations across the world – issues which threaten the stability of the global community almost more than anything else. It becomes very difficult to live in a global city without a car, or without shopping – participating in a global economy – which has its losers as well as its winners, or buying into mass consumerism, or to resist the privatisation of ethics and property.

In other words, we are no longer free to address the largest threats to our current existence, or to truly establish an alternative individual path. We are constrained to live this way whether we like it or not. Many are happy to blissfully go along with the tide, but we need to be aware that there is a tide, and that although we feel we are swimming freely, in fact we are being inexorably drawn in a particular direction. Taylor's analysis of the rise of the 'secular self' describes an increased sense of the individual, but a decreased sense of communal life, or power to act as a society to address issues of common concern. Individual freedom comes at a cost to social and shared values, where our disembedded lives, with no rootedness in a wider structure of existence, leave us powerless in the face of the larger forces shaping our world.

FREEDOM AND THE MARKET

The subjective turn in modern culture has led to a much wider range of possibilities for individuals but, if Taylor is right, it has also led to a loss of freedom in other areas of our life today. One of the engines driving our sense that we have greater freedom today is the existence of consumer choice. Wander into any supermarket or department store and the range of choice is remarkable, unimaginable to even our parents and grandparents. I can choose any brand of breakfast cereal, a dizzying array of items of clothing, a different watch for each day of the week, and any arrangement I can possibly think of for the furnishings of my home (if I can afford it, that is). Surely choice means freedom?

Yet does it? A number of voices are increasingly arguing that the multiplication of choice paradoxically diminishes our freedom rather than enhancing it. In *The Paradox of Choice,* Barry Schwartz argues that there comes a tipping point at which too much choice inhibits freedom, increases anxiety, and leads to psychological damage.[9] Outlining the explosion in consumer choice and varieties of options in our market-driven world, he argues that the ability to exercise some control over our environment is vital to well-being. The problem comes when the range of choices is so great, the pressure of deciding between them becomes so onerous, that we experience a loss of freedom rather than its enhancement.

For example, try buying a mobile phone today. First, you have to choose which brand of phone you want. Then you decide on the particular model, and whether to buy the latest, most expensive version, or go cheaper by buying last year's edition. Next, you have to choose the network provider – and you then are faced with a myriad of choices of different tariffs, bundles of free texts, minutes of call time, whether to go for the international roaming option, and so

---

[9] Schwartz, B. (2004), *The Paradox of Choice: Why More Is Less.* New York, HarperCollins.

on. The same is true when buying a pair of jeans, choosing a university or career, or even buying a house. There comes a point at which the range of choice is simply overwhelming. And even when the decision is made, the continued enticing range of choices can lead to doubt about whether you have chosen the right one, or even regret that you have made the wrong choice. Schwartz writes of the phenomenon of 'inaction inertia', where, faced with the pressure and burden of choice, people lapse into being unable to make any decision whatsoever.

In the course of his argument, he points out how sometimes it is precisely the restricting of options that leads to true freedom and contentment. Marriage, for example, entails a commitment to one person, and the decision to restrict one's affections and obligations to that person. It is a decision to close down one's options, and no longer pursue other emotional or sexual avenues. Yet all the studies seem to suggest that those who succeed in establishing a good, happy, stable marriage tend to be happier than those who do not. Buying a house is another. It actually restricts freedom by usually involving taking on huge debt, compelling the buyer to take and hold down a job over a long period to maintain the mortgage repayments. And yet most of us would prefer the security of owning our own home to the 'freedom' of renting or even being homeless.

Schwartz is a sociologist and psychologist, and this is a theory based on observation of contemporary life and consumer choice. A number of other sociologists and cultural theorists take a more analytical and historical approach. Zygmunt Bauman, like Charles Taylor, argues that the idea of the free individual, able to master their own fate, armed with free will, is not a universal phenomenon, but a social creation of modern capitalist societies. He argues that freedom in the modern sense of the word is essentially the freedom of the consumer, which, in consumer terms at least, requires and relies upon an effective market for goods. In the distant past, freedom simply meant emancipation from being dependent on the will of others – it meant freedom from slavery. It did not necessarily mean freedom to choose from a range of options.

In the absence of unequivocal norms in society, Bauman sees freedom of individual choice becoming more pronounced. To this extent, freedom is the result of uncertainty over where we fit into the world. A society where everyone is socially displaced from the rootedness in a social and geographical order leaves a great deal of choice to individuals. When the trajectory leads towards freedom from the demands of others, the logical end result is the avoidance of human contact with anyone other than our own chosen companions – the ultimate achievement of the super-wealthy, who can create their own private space, quite apart from others, undisturbed by the populace at large, or anyone who might have any kind of wider claim upon them. This kind of freedom has an obvious downside. It does deliver independence, in that you no longer have to worry about the irritating demands of others upon you, but the price is isolation. As Bauman puts it: 'Abhorrence of oppression is balanced by dread of loneliness'.[10]

There are therefore a number of tensions at the heart of the modern dream of freedom. One is that we feel we need

[10] Bauman, Z. (1988), *Freedom*. Milton Keynes, Open University Press.

both individual freedom and human interaction, and yet one seems to militate against the other, at least in the libertarian tradition we examined in the last chapter.

Another lies in the results of consumer capitalism. An unrestrained and unregulated market initially enables the development of choice, allowing a million flowers to bloom, as a free market encourages innovation and entrepreneurial variety. Yet in the longer term, it tends to lead not to endless variety, but in fact to sameness. For example, in the IT world it is almost impossible to challenge the dominance of companies like Apple, Microsoft, Google, etc. Small companies developing their own IT solutions either get bought up by the large conglomerates or they simply fade away. What is out of the question is going head-to-head with one of these giants and winning. In many spheres of consumerism, certain brands become dominant, increasing the pressure on individuals to wear, eat, drink, play with those brands as a sign of social acceptance and success.

The other side of this is the trend towards independence. In reaction to the dominance of certain brands, there is the backlash – the preference for independent chains of coffee shops, bookstores, clothing lines and the like. Yet even here, the promise of freedom is not so straightforward. Freedom in this sphere means having to construct your own social identity by the careful choice of what defines and expresses your inner self. There is a degree of freedom in this, but it also involves fear and self-doubt, the anxiety that others may not approve of your own individual choices. What if your friends don't like your new outfit or hairstyle? As Bauman puts it (a little more philosophically), 'self-construction of the self is a necessity; self-confirmation of the self is an impossibility'.[11] He argues that while in previous ages it was our work that defined us, today it is consumer choice that is central to contemporary self-definition. We are what we buy. Our consumer choices define us because they announce to others the kind of person we are, and the group we belong to. There is a quiet but undeniable pressure to spend, to buy the latest version of car, laptop, phone, Xbox, etc. but it is never felt as pressure. It is always presented as choice – the joy of preparing food from this particular cookbook, or driving that particular car – but it is pressure nonetheless. The needs of consumers are driven by advertisers and marketing professionals, not the other way round.

FREEDOM AND THE FUTURE

The result of all this is a profound sense of the lack of freedom in contemporary life. We assume we have untrammelled individual freedom, but in fact our choices are often restricted to the goods chosen for us by the most powerful and persuasive marketing campaigns. Capitalism boasts freedom of choice, and yet often tends towards the narrowing of that choice to a few corporate options. The desire to be free from the demands of others leads inexorably to isolation and loneliness, or the creation of enclosed communities of the like-minded, just like gated communities which keep out those who are different or embarrassing.

John Gray is one of the most influential and widely read political theorists and cultural commentators of our day. In particular, he is sceptical about the common idea that freedom is something that naturally arises when state

[11] Ibid., p.62.

repression is removed. Instead, 'freedom is an extremely complicated and delicate construction that can be maintained only by making continuous adjustments … Politics is the art of choosing between rival freedoms'.[12] The idea that we are progressing to an age of freedom, perhaps as a result of the expansion of Western democracy to other parts of the world, is a simple teleological mistake: 'Freedom is recurrently won and lost in an alternation that includes long periods of anarchy and tyranny, and there is no reason to suppose that this cycle will ever end'.[13]

In his book *The Soul of the Marionette* Gray plays with the image of the graceful puppet, resistant to gravity, manipulated by strings, which has a kind of freedom because it is unaware of not being free. Like the first humans who ate from the tree of knowledge, self-awareness sets limits on freedom, in that it only increases a sense of the restrictions and earth-bound nature of human life. Gray raises the intriguing possibility, which we shall explore later in this book, of freedom not primarily as a form of relationship between human beings, but as 'a state of the soul in which conflict has been left behind'.[14]

For Gray, the predominant religion of modern life is a kind of scientific Gnosticism, which holds out the hope that scientific knowledge will give human beings an unparalleled freedom unknown to any former age. Romanticism held the belief that it could remake the world through the exercise of human will. In a similar vein, modern scientific rationalists (and it is hard to avoid the thought that

[12] Gray, J. (2004), *Heresies Against Progress and Other Illusions*. London, Granta, pp.109–10.
[13] Ibid., p.3.
[14] Gray, J. (2015), *The Soul of the Marionette: A Short Enquiry into Human Freedom*. London, Allen Lane, p.6.

he has in mind here the likes of Richard Dawkins) believe that knowledge is the key to freedom, and will one day free humanity from the chains of ignorance that bind it. For Gray, both Romanticism and modern Scientism are just pale imitations of the Christian narrative of salvation, but each with the fatal flaw that it fails to recognise the brokenness of human nature, which Christianity, with its doctrine of the fall, sees more clearly. As he put it in a previous work, 'in insisting that human nature is incorrigibly flawed, [Christianity] is far more realistic than the secular doctrines that followed it'.[15] His is a more pessimistic and gloomy version of the doctrine of sin, asserting that human beings are 'incorrigibly imperfect',[16] and ascribing our contemporary lack of realism to 'the resistance of a post-Christian age to the thought that we are flawed creatures whose lives will always contain evils'.[17]

Gray is profoundly sceptical about narratives that suggest the world is improving under the gentle tutelage of liberal humanism, marching towards a golden future of liberty proclaimed by politicians, scientists and cultural theorists. He cites the rise of the surveillance state as integral to globalisation. Ubiquitous security cameras, the ability of global IT corporations to track people through their mobile phones, the increased traces we now leave behind us through our texts, emails, tweets, Facebook posts and mobile phone calls, all conspire to create a

[15] Gray, J. (2004), *Heresies Against Progress and Other Illusions*. London, Granta, p.47.
[16] Classic orthodox Christian theology would agree that humankind is imperfect, but never entirely incorrigible.
[17] Gray, J. (1995), *Enlightenment's Wake: Politics and Culture at the Close of the Modern Age*. London, Routledge, p.18.

society in which nothing is private, everything is watched, and there is a degree of central control and surveillance beyond even the dreams of Jeremy Bentham's famous Panopticon, a social arrangement that enabled members of the community to be watched by central unseen authority, without ever knowing that they were being observed. Closed-circuit TV means increasingly that everything we do is watched. Social media deepens the sense that little is private any more, and mobile data harvesting by the companies that produce our phones and tablets means that they always, at least potentially, know where you are – hence the texts that ping on your phone, welcoming you to a new country when you cross a border, even if you have told no-one!

The personally customised mobile phone, that emblem of personal freedom, enabling you to speak to whoever you want, wherever and whenever you want, putting a vast range of information at your fingertips, releasing you from the limits of geography and space, at the same time allows potentially a far greater degree of social scrutiny and surveillance. It is a gilded cage into which we all happily walk, which gives freedom with one hand while taking it away with the other. This is a world in which everyone is known, and anonymity is increasingly rare. Although we live in a world that prides itself on championing individual liberty, we are probably at the same time one of the most closely supervised, monitored and regulated societies in human history.

The rise of robotics also promises a world in which machines replace humans. The likelihood is that we will develop machines that will think for themselves, and will be made in human likeness:

When thinking machines first arrive in the world they will be the work of flawed, intermittently lucid animals whose minds are stuffed with nonsense and delusion. In time …. matter – the true demiurge – will stir the mannequins into life. Mutating under the pressure of entropy, the machines humans have invented will develop faults and flaws of their own … Eventually these half-broken machines will have the impression that they are choosing their path through life. As in humans, this may be an illusion; but as the sensation takes hold, it will engender what in humans used to be called a soul.[18]

Gray's is a rather gloomy view of the modern world. Although not a Christian, he has a profound appreciation of the Christian narrative of fallen redemption, and sees most modern ideologies as pale imitations of that grand story. He also has a strong sense of the illusions of modern life, particularly the illusion of freedom. We are in one sense like the marionette, who thinks he is free, but is in fact pulled around by all kinds of forces beyond his control. However, in another sense we are worse off than the puppet, because we do not even have the illusion of freedom. Even if we were to create new forms of life ourselves, they would simply replicate the same flaw, the 'split in the self' that is characteristic of humanity.

We live in an age where the human and natural worlds increasingly coincide, so that human action is not somehow separate from nature, but has a profound impact on it, for example in the rise of global warming. The result is that as

---

[18] Gray, J. (2015), *The Soul of the Marionette: A Short Enquiry into Human Freedom*. London, Allen Lane, p.155.

our power over nature grows, paradoxically we become less in control. We cannot simply stop the process of climate change, which will continue to roll onwards regardless. We have destabilised the climate, made the planet less hospitable to ourselves and other forms of life, developed new destructive technologies which make it possible to destroy the very world upon which we depend, and now seem intent on replacing even ourselves. Smart machines are developing in such a way that eventually they will do much of our current work for us. Many jobs will be replaced by technology that can do them faster and more efficiently, and the result will be that many modern professions will go the way of the typing pool – into the oblivion of distant memory. John Gray thinks the only economic role left to most human beings will be that of consumers: 'that is all we will do to pass the time'.[19] He may be right; however, the history of 'labour-saving' devices suggests that, rather than increasing our freedom and leisure time, they in fact replace one set of tasks with another. The invention of email has led not to lots of free time, because we no longer have to write and send letters, but to a greater enslavement to the inbox!

In the face of this, Gray returns to his deep conviction of the incorrigibility of human nature. It is not so much free-dom or consciousness that makes us distinctively human, but inner turmoil – the fact that we experience so many conflicting desires that pull us in different directions – or what he calls the 'split in the self'.[20] He may have a strong sense of sin, as in Christian theology, but he has little idea

[19] Ibid., p.126.
[20] Ibid., p.153.

of ultimate salvation, believing that humankind will never overcome its basic limitations, and it is part of the hubris of modern philosophy and science that thinks it can.

Freedom, Gray believes, is not natural to us. It is something to be learnt and grown into: 'Freedom among humans is not a natural human condition. It is the practice of mutual non-interference – a rare skill that is slowly learnt and quickly forgotten. The purpose of this negative freedom is not to promote the evolution of humans into rational beings or to enable them to govern themselves; it is to protect human beings from each other'.[21] We simply have to accept our flaws and ignorance, and accepting that unknowing makes possible a kind of inner freedom, content to allow meaning to come and go: 'not looking to ascend into the heavens, they can find freedom in falling to earth'.[22]

Gray believes that freedom is never absolute, and can only be found through a delicate balance of liberties, where we acknowledge our own frailty, ignorance and prejudice, moderate our demands upon each other, and simply learn to put up with each other's differences. The best kind of freedom he can imagine is this 'mutual non-interference': a resolve to tolerate one another, and not get in each other's way.

The thinkers we have analysed in this chapter have all spotted that the emperor is wearing no clothes. Although we think we are free to choose, the reality is that those choices are far more circumscribed than we think, and we are encouraged in the illusion of free choice by the very forces that enslave us.

---

[21] Ibid., pp.161–2.
[22] Ibid., p.166.

Michel Foucault uncovers the hidden and subtle power dynamics at work in any given human interaction or culture. One might describe him as a cynic, and argue that he only deconstructs, rather than helps to build communities, which require the kind of trust that he tends to undermine. However, his analysis remains one of the most penetrating and influential accounts of the nature of institutions and their tendency to deceive with high-flying rhetoric about improvement, progress and freedom.

Zygmunt Bauman helps us see another aspect of the invisible web in which we are caught: the predominance of the market and its tendency to circumscribe our choices. Can any of us imagine work these days without a computer or a phone? If freedom means the genuine freedom to do as I wish, then my not being able to work without being tied to, even enslaved by, a keyboard and screen, or live without a mobile phone, represents the ultimate loss of freedom. To exist in the modern Western professional world without these gadgets is a concept almost impossible to understand today.

The illusion of freedom even extends to the brands we buy. I am typing this book on an Apple laptop. When I bought it, I had the impression that I was making a free choice, exercising my perfect consumer freedom to select a machine that would reflect my own lifestyle, work patterns and ideals. That all sounds fine, until I recognise that almost everyone else I know has made exactly the same choice, or if they haven't, they wish they had. Am I really as free to choose as I think? Was my decision to buy an Apple MacBook Air really an act of personal, unconditioned freedom? Or have I been subtly conditioned by years of marketing, peer pressure, careful image creation, into thinking that a progressive, contemporary person cannot really be seen without this accessory of the academic and professional life?

The paradox is that while our culture constantly markets individuality – the personalising of your phone, your desktop picture, your clothes – at the same time, there is no way out of the system. It is virtually impossible to live, or at least get a job, without the technology. Legislation increases daily to ensure nothing we do can go unrecorded, in case something goes wrong and we know who to blame. Companies monitor individual performance closely to maximise productivity and ensure compliance with external standards, to prevent damaging breaches of security or offending against regulatory powers, yet the result is an ever-decreasing arena for personal initiative and creativity.

When you add in the almost constant surveillance and scrutiny involved in modern life, the paradoxical loss of freedom which comes with the proliferation of choice, and the prospect of surrendering more and more of the range of human activity to intelligent machines, as envisaged by John Gray, then the suspicion grows: we are not as free as we think. You don't have to be an ardent Calvinist to believe that freedom is more of a myth than we imagine. Doctrines of predestination have always been common, either on theological grounds, for thinkers such as Augustine and Calvin, or for more strictly philosophical or biological reasons, as with philosophers such as Galen Strawson,[23] yet one does not have to enter complex theological or philosophical debates to gain a strong sense that our much-vaunted contemporary freedom is not as extensive as we thought.

[23] Strawson, G. (2010), *Freedom and Belief*. New York, OUP.

We are concluding on something of a downbeat note. We are certainly not free in the sense that the contemporary secular liberal consensus understands freedom – the freedom to choose what we want. This chapter has taken us on a tour of a number of recent voices pointing unerringly to the loss of freedom in contemporary life. There are, however, a number of other voices who begin to articulate a promise of something different. The next chapter looks at two such figures, who enable us to begin imagining an alternative kind of freedom.

4

Hints of Freedom

We ended the last chapter with a look at John Gray's analysis of freedom, which offered a robust critique of optimistic liberal trajectories of progress, and yet hinted at a way beyond the impasse suggestion by his definition of freedom as 'mutual non-interference'.

Gray's is a sobering vision, realistic and honest in its analysis of human frailty, and refusing to be lulled by the false promises of hubristic scientific or political visions. At the same time it is perhaps a rather limited and slightly depressing outlook. The vision of freedom as 'mutual non-interference' seems to imply a rather atomised form of social life, where each individual pursues their own vision, negotiating provisional compromises when that way of life bumps into others, rather than a more hopeful vision of communal coherence. It is a vision of muddling along somehow, enjoying life while one can, but without any particular direction or trajectory.

Before we move on to Christian theology and the resources it brings to a renewed vision of freedom, there are a number of other voices outside, or on the fringes of, Christianity that point in a new direction. This chapter looks at two of them.

IRIS MURDOCH

Like John Gray, whom we met in the last chapter, the novelist and philosopher Iris Murdoch was a sceptic when it came to some of the more optimistic and confident predictions of human-centred progress. Also like Gray, she writes consciously of the disappearance of religion, and what she considers the impossibility of its return in the modern or post-modern world. Murdoch cannot bring herself to believe in God, yet is haunted by his absence. As her biographer Peter Conradi comments: 'She thought the disappearance or weakening of religion the most important thing that has happened to us over the past hundred years'.[1]

Despite her location in Oxford, she increasingly moved away from the Oxford analytical school dominant in philosophy in her own time, largely because of her continued interest in and fascination with what were at heart theological questions. In a number of her writings, she analyses closely and perceptively the idea of freedom, particularly in relation to some of the other contemporary philosophical conceptions of it. She returns often to the formulation of freedom she finds particularly unconvincing: freedom as essentially the exercise of the will. She was deeply attracted to the idea of, not so much God, as the reality and objectivity of the Good. Reacting against thinkers of her own time such as Stuart Hampshire, who argued that the existence of goodness as a fixed, objective reality inhibited the freedom of human beings, she increasingly focused attention upon the primacy of the inner, long-term trajectory of the self, rather than the individual, isolated act of choice, as the true

---

[1] Conradi, P. (2001), *Iris Murdoch: A Life*. New York, Norton, p.587.

exercise of freedom. She thought the philosophical origins of this mistake lay in Wittgenstein's impatience with the idea of inner decisions which never issue in action. This frustration was perfectly fine as far as it went, but existentialist and utilitarian philosophers had built upon it to argue that an inner change of heart or mind is meaningless: the only significant thing is our own decision and action. In this view, freedom was therefore the exercise of the sovereign human will in a particular moment, doing just as it happened to choose.

The metaphor she uses to explain this view of moral action is that of shopping. The customer enters the store, surveys the various products on offer, and rationally and freely chooses from the goods displayed before him. On this view, moral action is a choice made objectively and in a particular moment, as a pure act of will. If the customer happens to feel like cake as opposed to apples, then she simply chooses cake as an act of pure will. This of course reflects the popular contemporary existentialism of the 1960s, which emphasised the solitary omnipotent will over any sense of inner character or conditions of heart and mind. On this view, only outward moral action counts. What is chosen matters less than the fact of choice itself. We simply analyse and try to acquire as full a knowledge of the situation facing us as possible, and then make a choice on that basis. This is an absolute focus on the importance of will, 'isolated from belief, from reason, from feeling … the essential centre of the self'.[2] This is freedom exercised as an absolute, a choice made out of the blue, as an expression of sheer volition.

---

[2] Murdoch, I. (1971a), *The Sovereignty of Good*. London, Routledge & Kegan Paul, p.7.

This individual, making free choices as an isolated individual, uninfluenced by the inner currents of character formation or of emotion, is, Murdoch thinks, the hero of most contemporary novels (at least it was in the 1960s when she was writing). In fact, she says, his origins go back some way before that, to Kant. She is worth quoting at length to grasp her analysis of the genealogy of this view of freedom:

Kant abolished God and made man God, in his stead. We are still living in the age of the Kantian man, or Kantian man-god. Kant's conclusive exposure of the so-called proofs of the existence of God, his analysis of the limitations of speculative reason, together with his eloquent portrayal of the dignity of rational man, has had results which might possibly dismay him. How recognisable, how familiar to us, is the man so beautifully portrayed in the *Grundlegung* who, confronted even with Christ, turns away to consider the judgement of his own conscience and to hear the voice of his own reason. Stripped of the exiguous metaphysical background which Kant was prepared to allow him, this man is still with us, free, independent, lonely, powerful, rational, responsible, brave, the hero of so many novels and books of moral philosophy. The *raison d'être* of this attractive but misleading creature is not too far to seek. He is the offspring of the age of science, confidently rational and yet increasingly aware of his alienation from the material universe which his discoveries reveal; and since he is not a Hegelian (Kant, not Hegel, has provided Western ethics with its dominating image) his alienation is without cure. He is the ideal citizen of the liberal state, a warning held up to tyrants. He has the virtue which the age requires and admires: courage. It is not such a very long step from Kant to Nietzsche, and from Nietzsche to existentialism, and the Anglo-Saxon ethical doctrines which in some ways closely resemble it. In fact, Kant's man had already received a glorious incarnation a century earlier in the work of Milton; his proper name is Lucifer.[3]

This Kantian individual assumes that the instant of decision is everything. Shorn of belief in (or at least certainty about) God, or a deep connection with the physical universe, the individual is left in heroic isolation, free to act on his own whim, sure of the absoluteness of his freedom. The reference to *Paradise Lost* is striking. This is the morally detached, independent individual who will never yield to anyone else's will, for whom the exercise of personal will is the paramount value. It is indeed Lucifer, the one who says:

What though the field be lost?
All is not lost; the unconquerable will,
And study of revenge, immortal hate,
And courage never to submit or yield:
That glory never shall his wrath or might
Extort from me. To bow and sue for grace
With suppliant knee, and deify his power,
Who from the terror of this arm so late
Doubted his empire, that were low indeed
That were an ignominy and shame beneath
This downfall ...[4]

[3] Ibid., p.78.
[4] *Paradise Lost* I. 105–116.

The last thing he will do is to bow the knee to God, or anyone else for that matter. Hell may not be pleasant, but at least there he defers to no-one. As he declares later in the epic poem:

> Here we reign secure, and in my choice
> To reign is worth ambition though in Hell
> Better to reign in Hell, than serve in Heaven.[5]

In contrast to this sovereign individual making decisions out of the pure moment of personal liberty, Murdoch thinks that good choices arise out of longer habits of life, a steady attention to practices that purify the soul, and in particular the ability to see well and clearly. While both Kant and Hume 'abhor history', time matters, because it is over time that moral capacity develops. She emphasises the inner not the outer, the substantial self, not the isolated individual. However, this is a self that is developed not by introspection, but by the steady gaze at something outside itself. In Murdoch's world, the individual is not alone. She is drawn not so much to God, but to concepts such as the good, or love, or beauty. 'The central concept of morality is the individual knowable by love.'[6] She has in mind 'the endless aspiration to perfection which is characteristic of moral activity'.[7]

Introspection, looking inside at the self, is fruitless. We become so wrapped up in ourselves, finding ourselves so dazzling, that we are able to see nothing else. Instead, she suggests, we 'grow by looking'. For Iris Murdoch the characteristic act of the human being is not much the free,

---

[5] Ibid, I. 261–263.
[6] Murdoch, I. (1971a), *The Sovereignty of Good*. London, Routledge & Kegan Paul, p.40.
[7] Ibid., p.30.

existential, arbitrary choice of the individual, but the act of paying attention to something outside of and better than oneself. 'Our ability to act well, when the time comes, depends upon the quality of our habitual objects of attention.'[8] Moral change and achievement are by necessity slow. We cannot simply alter ourselves, and we make good choices not by individual acts of will, but through slow, steady learning to see and desire the good. In fact, the final and desirable condition for moral action is a kind of necessity, whereby a person sees the good so clearly that there is no real choice to make – the right path is simply obvious. In this condition, true freedom again looks like a kind of obedience. The moral agent is 'compelled by obedience to the reality he can see'.[9] This is a condition that only saints and artists know well. It is a decidedly ascetic vision of freedom, one which is not assumed, but striven for; not a given, but an aspiration.

Here we begin to see a very different understanding of freedom. Murdoch is deeply dissatisfied with and unconvinced by the existentialist–behaviourist self, simply free to choose as a mere act of will. Such a self assumes that there are no other conditions affecting the choice. She is far too astute an observer of human behaviour to buy that.

In summary, for Iris Murdoch, freedom is not the expression of self, or the ability to simply choose what one wants: it is 'a disciplined overcoming of self'.[10] It becomes a kind of compulsion: when you see the beauty and desirability of the good, then freedom is the compulsion to choose that good, because why would you want to do anything else? Presumably it is possible to reject goodness, but then that displays a form

[8] Ibid., p.55.
[9] Ibid., p.40.
[10] Ibid., p.93.

of perversity or, more charitably, a lack of vision; a refusal to see the attractiveness, the desirability of goodness.

Like John Gray, Iris Murdoch has a strong sense of what Christians would call human sinfulness. Although she has no belief in God, she does have a sense of sin, what she calls a kind of fantasy, 'the proliferation of blinding self-centred aims and images'.[11] Once we have a sense that all is not well in the human soul, then the image of freedom as the mere exercise of will becomes problematic. You might be free to do what you want, but what if 'what you want' is precisely the problem? She shares Gray's pessimism about basic human nature, and his scepticism that we have the inherent moral ability to make good choices, and progress towards a kind of social nirvana. Like him, she also sees freedom as something to be learnt, and grown into, rather than something that can be assumed. However, her version of freedom goes beyond Gray's in offering a slightly more hopeful vision of transformation. Due to her Platonic conception of the good, towards which our mental and spiritual attention is to be directed, she does offer a richer and more hopeful vision of change than Gray, with his more limited prospect of mere 'mutual non-interference.' God may have disappeared from the world, but He can perhaps be replaced by the good, a more impersonal concept, perhaps less demanding of faith.

But can He? The belief in goodness, without an objective grounding in God, means that we humans are dealing with and oriented towards an impersonal entity, something which somehow feels less than ourselves. Murdoch ends up simply asserting the existence of goodness, which leaves the

[11] Ibid., p.65.

question: if you just assert the existence of goodness, why it is impossible to just assert the existence of God? Once you have taken the metaphysical step towards asserting the objective reality of 'goodness', then it is not too far to take the further step towards recognising the personal nature and origin of goodness. In fact, we might argue that such a step is necessary, as an impersonal goodness is somehow less concrete, imaginable and desirable than goodness which has a personal origin and a personal end.

Murdoch is fascinated by and drawn to the saints and the ascetics in their devotion to the good, but of course the Christian mystics themselves would have gone beyond the idea of the good, to an insistence on attachment to and contemplation of a personal God, as revealed in the very incarnation of goodness, Jesus Christ. In her essay 'On "God" and "Good"', she considers models of goodness such as Christ or Socrates, but concludes that 'the information about them is scanty and vague',[12] thus leading her to avoid a proper attention to Christ, for example, as the personal incarnation of goodness. She was, perhaps, a victim of her age, of the fashionable 1960s scepticism about the historical Jesus, fuelled by Rudolf Bultmann's reading of the New Testament, which infected much British biblical scholarship, and was ironically inspired by the very existentialism that Murdoch repudiated.[13] Today's biblical scholarship is much more confident of access to historical data about Christ that restores the opportunity for serious engagement

---

[12] Ibid., p.51.
[13] For a while in the late 1940s and early 1950s, Iris Murdoch attended meetings of the High Anglican group in Oxford called the 'Metaphysicals', one of the leading voices of which was Dennis Nineham, one of the most avid British followers and interpreters of Rudolf Bultmann. See Conradi, P. (2001), *Iris Murdoch: A Life*. New York, Norton, p.306.

with the possibility of both incarnation and revelation.[14] In these early years Murdoch was allergic to the supernatural, but strangely credulous when it came to the paranormal, which begs the question of whether she is being entirely consistent in asserting goodness while denying its personal origin in the transcendent realm and the possibility of its incarnation in history. Asserting the magnetism and reality of goodness, yet denying its personal origin, makes it much harder to imagine it taking personal form in us. Peter Conradi's perceptive comment was that her vision is 'surreptitiously dependent ... on the theology it is designed to supplant'.[15] In later works, such as *Metaphysics as a Guide to Morals*, published in 1992, she moved away from her 1960s certainty about the foolishness of believing in God, to not exactly believing herself, but finding it possible to believe that others might reasonably believe.[16] The arguments there are less assertive of the impossibility of belief in God as opposed to goodness, and sometimes slip into, for example, defences of the validity of prayer and the importance of religious instruction. The tension between her assertion of the role of goodness and her contrasting assertion that God is out of date is still there, but less confident than it was in *The Sovereignty of Good*.

Iris Murdoch points us to a vision of freedom as finding something good on which to focus attention. Freedom is not the liberty to assert our own naked choices, but a form of obedience to something outside ourselves, something which is inherently desirable.

---

[14] For example: Bauckham, R. (2006), *Jesus and the Eyewitnesses: the Gospels as Eyewitness Testimony*. Grand Rapids, Mich.; Cambridge, Eerdmans.
[15] Conradi, P. (2001), *Iris Murdoch: A Life*. New York, Norton, p.477.
[16] Murdoch, I. (2003), *Metaphysics as a Guide to Morals*. London, Vintage.

SIMONE WEIL

One figure who influenced Iris Murdoch deeply, and whose thought on freedom was both creative and original, and had some parallels with Murdoch's, was Simone Weil, the French philosopher, activist and mystic. Writing in the 1930s, with Europe deeply divided between the Communist east, and the growth of fascism in Western Europe, she was one of the most significant intellectual and spiritual thinkers of the twentieth century. Only 34 when she died, in part due to a punishing regime of ascetic abstinence from food, at least in part in solidarity with victims in German-occupied France, and partly due to long-term frailty, she too reflected deeply on the nature of freedom and oppression. Although born into a secular family, she was led by a number of powerful experiences in her later life to a profound and mystical religious faith, even if of a rather unconventional type.

Her early thinking on this topic focused on politics. In her 'Reflections Concerning the Causes of Liberty and Social Oppression', published in 1934, she explored the nature and possibility of a free society. The Marxist dream, very current and attractive to many in those inter-war years, was of a state where technology made production virtually effortless, removing the ancient curse of work. However, for Weil this was an illusion, or at least something which missed a vital component of freedom, which is that it can only be acquired through overcoming certain obstacles. Freedom is not an absence of work or necessity; it is instead something to be learnt as a disciplined activity. It is not so much a relationship between desire and satisfaction, the ability to satisfy our desires, as a relationship between thought and action. In other words, it is not the condition whereby we can get what we want without any great effort. It is not, as commonly assumed, the freedom simply to choose for yourself, to get what you find pleasurable without having to try too hard. It is instead what happens when the mind begins to be able to master the body. It is, borrowing the language of Hegel, 'the body, rendered as it were fluid through habit'.[17] Freedom only comes from the disciplined application of the powers of mind and body, moving beyond mere desire and 'vain fears', to the development of moderation and courage, virtues essential for a functioning social life. Freedom is a kind of self-mastery, a state where 'the material conditions that enable [an individual] to exist were exclusively the work of his mind directing the effort of his muscles. This would be true liberty'.[18]

Weil thinks of freedom as a skill to be learnt, not an assumption to be made. It is a kind of adaptability, whereby the mind masters the body to accomplish the tasks which need to be done to make a community function well. It is a kind of skill whereby the body has become so used to certain actions that it does them through habit, almost by necessity. The existence of other people, in some views of freedom, and particularly in the libertarian tradition we examined in chapter two, is potentially an obstacle to individual liberty. However, a truly free society, argues Weil, is one where everyone exercises their own individual freedom and reason for the achievement of a *common* task. Work is not an unfortunate necessity, which true freedom would eliminate (many a lottery winner, imagining the freedom it would hopefully bring, has thrown in their job to spend

---

[17] Weil, S. (2001), *Oppression and Liberty*. London, Routledge, p.86.
[18] Ibid., p.83.

their winnings on endless holidays), but is instead a positive good – a conscious submission to necessity. Work becomes essential to spiritual development.

During the 1930s, having left her job as a teacher, Weil made a decision to go and work in a factory, at a Renault auto plant. She later attributed her spiritual education to this mechanical work. It seemed to her that this submission to working in a purely mechanical process became a kind of emblem of the spiritual life. The natural condition of humanity, she considers, is just as she experienced it in that factory: 'an obedience to mechanical laws as blind and as exact as the laws of gravitation'.[19] This vision is shaped by her deep sense of the repressive totalitarianism of Europe in the 1930s, but it is not just that: her sense of the necessity in which human beings are bound extends into a more universal sense that, as we explored in the last chapter, our choices may be much more limited than we think. We have limited freedom to move or to act: in fact, the only choice we have is in which direction we look.

After a period in Spain, in support of the loyalists in the Spanish Civil War, Weil returned to France and began to undergo a kind of religious conversion. A combination of the experience of listening to Gregorian chant at a moment of severe migraine, and reading the English metaphysical poets such as George Herbert, brought on an intense fascination with the exploration of God, affliction, love and necessity. Her sense of the routine necessity of manual work, and the overcoming of obstacles it requires, was gathered up in a new sense of direction, a new goal to be pursued, beyond the idea of a functioning society; into a desire for something more.

---

[19] Weil, S. (2009), *Waiting for God*. New York, Harper Perennial, p.75.

Towards the end of her life, Simone Weil became fascinated with God, as the great object of desire and attention, although she always had difficulties with the church, to the extent that she chose never to be baptised, feeling a mixture of unworthiness and distaste for what she called the 'social structure' of the institution. From her earlier thinking she retained a strong sense of the constraints upon humanity and the limits placed on us in our embodied condition. We are the subjects of a 'blind mechanism' which tosses us around, and the only option is whether to look towards God or away from him. So, for example, she writes: 'as for us, we are nailed down to the spot, only free to choose which way we look, ruled by necessity'.[20] Or, in another image, 'we are like plants that have the one choice of being in or out of the light'.[21]

She considered God's act of creation as an act of divine withdrawal – the leaving of a space where God is not. Human beings inhabit this space, which is the place of the absence of God. The true goal of human life, lived in this space, therefore, is not so much to walk towards God, as God cannot be seen or touched in this life, but to be oriented towards him. Our condition is inevitably linked to this absent God: 'Men can never escape from obedience to God. A creature cannot but obey. The only choice given to men, as intelligent and free creatures, is to desire obedience or not to desire it. If a man does not desire it, he obeys nevertheless, perpetually, inasmuch as he is a thing subject to mechanical necessity'.[22]

[20] Ibid., p.73.
[21] Ibid., p.77.
[22] Ibid., p.76.

As for Iris Murdoch, freedom comes, not by the exercise of personal choice, but by orienting ourselves towards something outside ourselves – only now the object of attention is God, not just goodness. A pure materialism which is content merely with the physical is death. Weil's writing towards the end of her life is permeated with this desire for God, often nurtured by affliction, which for her is a deeper and more spiritually aware form of suffering. In this space, the art of living is not so much to achieve, or to construct great things, but to learn to pay attention in the right direction.

In fact, the concept of attention is central to her understanding of the spiritual life. In a brief piece entitled 'Reflections on the Right Use of School Studies with a View to the Love of God', she argues that 'the development of the faculty of attention forms the real object and almost the sole interest of studies'.[23] The point of learning Greek, French, mathematics, or indeed any discipline, is not so much the object of the study itself, but the development of the faculty of attention, so that it can be ultimately directed towards God as the true object of desire and prayer: 'Attention animated by desire is the whole foundation of religious practices.'[24]

Freedom therefore comes not in an act or through the exercise of personal will (in this she deeply influenced Iris Murdoch), but from looking in the right direction:

God has provided that when his grace penetrates to the very centre of a man and from there illuminates his being, he is able to walk on the water without violating

[23] Ibid., p.57.
[24] Ibid., p.129.

any of the laws of nature. When, however, a man turns away from God, he simply gives himself up to the law of gravity. Then he thinks that he can decide and choose, but he is only a thing, a stone that falls.[25]

Turning away from God results not in liberty from the shackles of divine command, but in slavery to the inevitability of being trapped in the mechanisms of human society and behaviour. God is the source of all being, and so the desire for God is a kind of upward force that pulls a person towards the light, a magnetic attraction that lifts a person upwards, rather than their merely falling passively downwards to destruction. Physical matter, apparently inert, docile and inactive, yet moulded and shaped by its Creator, is a picture of what human life can be and is meant to be. The sea is beautiful because it is passive, perfectly obedient to the action of gravity and the pull of the tides. In the same way, human beings become beautiful when they too are drawn towards and responsive to the movement of God.

Weil's thought is sometimes seen as a kind of Stoic Christianity. For her, acceptance of necessity is vital for freedom. Rather than trying to change the world, true freedom comes from an acceptance of the value of obedience and necessity. Ultimately everything obeys necessity – some do it willingly and with consent, some in ignorance and falsehood. Freedom means encouraging obedience as a spiritual discipline, a kind of active obedience to the way things are, so that, as in Iris Murdoch, obedience is the only true freedom. Refusal of necessity only results in sinking down in gravity, like a falling stone. Choosing to turn away from the

---

[25] Ibid., p.75.

source of all goodness, from the author of Love, is in fact to limit oneself, to restrict human possibilities.

Whereas thinkers like Locke, Rousseau and Mill saw freedom as liberation from restraints, Simone Weil sees it arising out of an active acceptance of limitation. Freedom is paradoxically a form of voluntary obedience, a pliability in the hands of God, which is the ultimate goal of humanity: 'I want nothing else but obedience, obedience itself, in its totality'.[26] Practising a trade can be a means of understanding obedience; a kind of apprenticeship, which requires time and effort.[27] It is something to be learned, because it requires this focused, determined attention, an intense 'Waiting for God'. Obedience to God is placing oneself in 'the current of supreme Good',[28] allowing oneself to be carried by the river of attraction towards the God of Love.

Obedience is the supreme virtue: a loving necessity, which is action motivated purely by love of God. Love of necessity is love of what happens to you whatever it may be, because that is the result of God's decision to create.[29] 'Consent to necessity alone makes a human being free.'[30]

However freedom may start in attention to God, it flows out into relations with the world. God is not, at the end of the day, to be the sole object of attention, in the same way that we don't just look at a light but at the things which it illuminates. So, this attentiveness to God issues in care for the creatures God has made and given. Saintliness is seen

---

[26] Ibid., p.15
[27] Ibid., p.78
[28] Weil, S. (1952), *The Need for Roots*. Abingdon, Routledge, p.296.
[29] See McCullough, L. (2014), *The Religious Philosophy of Simone Weil*. London, I.B. Tauris. Chapter 4.
[30] Ibid., p.222.

not in what a person says about God, but in how they see and treat the things of this world. Care for creatures is therefore the one verifiable expression of love for God.

Simone Weil's thought, a complex, mystical blend of politics, philosophy, theology and spiritual insight, has often been seen as one of the most perceptive commentaries on the twentieth-century malaise in European culture. As already mentioned, Weil was a significant influence on Iris Murdoch. When she read Weil's *The Need for Roots* in 1947, she gained from it a way of thinking that reinforced her sense that the self needs to be de-centred, displaced outside itself. Both writers have a common intuition that true freedom does not exist in a vacuum, neither is it an act of the sovereign will, but derives from steady attention to something, or someone, greater and better than the hopelessly compromised self.

Both thinkers have an interest in meditation and prayer,[31] yet Weil's object of attention, unlike Murdoch's, is intensely personal. Her attention is fixed not upon the Platonic abstraction of 'the Good', but on a God who has addressed her. Unlike Iris Murdoch, she came to see desire for the good as essentially a religious quest. For her there is no such thing as secular morality, because we cannot be or do good without receiving good from some transcendent source outside ourselves. Created things, like sticks to a drowning man, cannot bear the weight of our longing. Goodness does not have its source in this world, and the way to acceptance is to detach desire from changeable objects and attach it to whatever, or whoever, is unconditionally good. Only by

---

[31] Murdoch has the delightful phrase that 'prayer is an attention to God which is a form of love': Murdoch, I. (1971b), *The Sovereignty of Good*. London, Routledge, pp.53–4.

reaching for ultimate goodness, which is God, can we be freed from reaching for what will inevitably turn to dust in our hands.[32] For Weil, this attention towards the good becomes a conversation, a person meeting the Person, which ultimately gives it a more satisfying and compelling force. With Simone Weil, we get the sense of an encounter with a warm-blooded, living being rather than a slightly cold and abstract form.

This chapter has brought us face-to-face with two key thinkers of recent times, who share a scepticism about the idea that our goal as human beings should be to be free to choose whatever we want, and indeed that the world is waiting for the exercise of our pure sovereign wills on an inert and objective world. Instead, they envisage freedom in different terms, as something gradually learnt, rather than merely assumed. At the same time, in the progression of the chapter, we have seen an increasing focus on the importance of freedom as derived from an orientation to something outside itself. Freedom all depends on what you're looking at. For both Iris Murdoch and Simone Weil, freedom and obedience are not opposites, but in fact belong together. We will revisit these ideas, but now it is time to delve into the Christian tradition of thinking on freedom, as we begin to explore how theologians have envisaged, experienced and described the elusive gift of freedom.

---

[32] As Lissa McCullough puts it: 'Only by directing our longing to the pure good, or God, can we escape reaching for things that turn to death and futility in our grasp.' McCullough, L. (2014), *The Religious Philosophy of Simone Weil*. London, I.B. Tauris, p.67.

5

The Apostle of Freedom

Having sketched some of the contours and history of our views of freedom, and begun to see some hints of a different kind, it is high time we turned towards something else. In this section of the book we will look at what a Christian view of freedom has to offer the modern world. Our task is to lay foundations by looking at some key figures in Christian history who have thought long and hard about freedom and, in the course of that thinking, offer us a take on liberty and how it works radically different from some of the secular models we have seen so far.

As the gospels report him, Jesus himself spoke of freedom several times, including the choice of a key Old Testament text – Isaiah 61 – at the announcement of the start of his public ministry in his hometown of Nazareth:

The Spirit of the Lord is on me, because he has anointed me to preach good news to the poor. He has sent me to proclaim freedom for the prisoners, and recovery of sight for the blind, to release the oppressed, to proclaim the year of the Lord's favour. (Lk. 4.18–19)

The word here (used twice) is not the usual Greek word for freedom, *eleutheros*, but the word *aphesis*, which has more of a sense of release from captivity, or pardon from punishment. *Eleutheros*, which occurs only in John's gospel, has a more distinct political and social connotation, including the idea of personal or social independence – being free as opposed to being a slave, the state of freedom rather than the act of being freed. In John, Jesus proclaims that the 'truth will make you free' (8.32), and that 'if the Son makes you free, you will be free indeed' (8.36). Other than that, the idea of political or social freedom is not prominent in the gospel accounts of the teaching of Jesus. The one place where it could be said to be is in his actions. The miracle stories are essentially accounts of release from bondage – the common bondage of sickness and disability in a world without health care or social security. That the Greek word most commonly used to refer to freedom in the synoptic gospels is *aphesis* rather than *eleutheros* points us already towards an idea of freedom with a different tone. This is freedom as release from bondage, from that which denies people fullness of life, or freedom from captivity. *Aphesis* is also the word commonly used for release from the captivity of sin.[1] Perhaps the ideas of forgiveness and freedom are not as far apart as sometimes appear.

The one New Testament figure who builds most constructively on this theme of freedom and release is of course St Paul.

A strong argument has recently been made that Paul marks a massive turn in Western thought, from a world

---

[1] For example in Matthew 26.28, Mark 1.4, Luke 1.77, 3.3, 24.47, Acts 2.38, 5.31 and many other times in the epistles.

where natural inequality between persons was simply assumed, where freedom was enjoyed by some but not by most, to one in which freedom for every individual, regardless of social status, became conceivable. Larry Siedentop's *Inventing the Individual* makes the argument that although we tend to see society as a collection of individuals, it wasn't always that way.[2] Originally the ancient world was dominated by the family, with the primary religious duty of honouring ancestors and the absolute authority of the patriarchal figure who stood at the head of each family. The crucial distinction in such a world was not between private and public realms, but between the public and the domestic. Wider associations subsequently emerged, as various tribes came together, recognising a common ancestor, to create cities. In the rise of the Greek city-state, loyalty was transferred from the family to the city and its gods. Patriotism, patriarchy and piety were all therefore closely intertwined with each other. Liberty in this context meant the freedom to have a share in government, and a say in public policy, a privilege available to free men, but not to slaves. Citizens were necessarily superior to other men, endowed with reason and a desire for honour. A just society was governed by reason, and therefore the most rational of men, the philosophers, were those naturally assumed to be most fit to govern. In all of this, it was clear that the individual *per se* had no particular standing. Identity came from belonging to the family, the tribe or the city, not from any inherent rights held by the individual person. In this world, the demand was not to be true to yourself, but to be true to your tribe.

[2] Siedentop, L. (2014), *Inventing the Individual: The Origins of Western Liberalism.* London, Allen Lane.

All this began to change with the decline of the independent city-state under the growing imperial power of first Alexander the Great and then the Romans, which served to erode this common sense of civic loyalty and belonging. As Rome evolved from a republic into an empire, and cities across the Mediterranean basin and beyond lost their independence to become part of this expanding empire, local identities weakened, paving the way for a new form of social interaction. The architect and instigator of this new way of relating in society, according to Siedentop, was none other than St Paul himself. For him, moral agency was potentially available to all individuals, not just freemen or philosophers. The new basis for social association was voluntary, with people coming together to form these new communities called churches, associations based not in nature, ethnicity or social status, but in the distinct call to love one another in the name of Christ. These were communities in which being 'Greek or Jew, circumcised or uncircumcised, barbarian, Scythian slave or free'[3] counted for nothing – Christ was all and in all. This vision began to give birth to the free individual, liberated from the demands of loyalty to family, tribe, city or ethnic identity, as well as to the more sinister spiritual forces at work in the metaphysical realm. Paul assumes the human capacity to think and to choose, arguing that freedom and autonomy is only found through an act of submission, to the will and mind of God in Christ. In other words, Paul 'wagers on human equality'.[4]

It is a simple and elegant argument that points to the significance of St Paul in articulating a new view of freedom

---

[3] Colossians 3.11.

[4] Siedentop, L. (2014), *Inventing the Individual: The Origins of Western Liberalism*. London, Allen Lane, p.60.

in place of that of the ancient world. If it has any truth, we would need to dig a little deeper than Siedentop is able to do in his rather brief treatment of St Paul, to see how and why freedom is such a key idea in his writings, and what he means by it. Not only that, but our task here is to discover the lines of agreement and disagreement between Christian views of freedom and, not so much antiquity, but modernity. If St Paul offers a radically new view of freedom from Greek and Roman thought, does he also offer something different from modern Western approaches to freedom?

PAUL THE APOCALYPTIC PROPHET

This is not the place for an extended discussion of recent interpretations of Pauline theology, but those in any way familiar with Pauline scholarship will know of the debate between what is often called the 'Old Perspective on Paul', normally associated with the classic Lutheran understanding of the apostle and his gospel, and the 'New Perspective', associated with figures such as E.P. Sanders, James Dunn, N.T. Wright and many others.[5] In recent times, a new reading of St Paul has emerged which moves beyond both old and new perspectives, and focuses on the apocalyptic aspects of Paul's thinking.[6]

One of the key figures in this movement is Douglas Campbell, whose book *The Deliverance of God*[7] has caused

---

[5] For an account of how Luther might not be as far away from the 'New Perspective' as is sometimes thought, see Tomlin, G. (2017), *Luther's Gospel: Reimagining the World*. London, Bloomsbury, Chapter 3.

[6] Tilling, C., (2014), 'Beyond Old and New Perspectives on Paul: Reflections on the Work of Douglas Campbell.' 341. Eugene, Or.: Cascade.

[7] Campbell, D. (2009), *The Deliverance of God: an Apocalyptic Rereading of Justification in Paul*. Grand Rapids, Eerdmans.

quite a stir in the circles of those who read Paul closely. The key idea at the heart of Paul's gospel, according to Campbell's reading of it, is that God has acted in Christ and the sending of the Holy Spirit to bring deliverance to the human race. The primary dialectic in St Paul – what Campbell calls 'Justification Theory' – opposing being sinful to being righteous, being 'unjustified' to being 'justified', concerns the difference between being under slavery and being free. Paul's gospel is not a two-phase contract, with the first the law – as a rigorous one demanding obedience and moral perfection, which proves impossible to achieve, and the second – the gospel – a softer one by which God provides forgiveness for failure to meet the demands of the law. Instead there is a single covenant: the announcement of a new age of liberation for the human race. This is not so much a retributive as an apocalyptic reading, which focuses attention on the shift of eras or aeons, from the old age of Adam to the new age of Christ. In the past, under Adam, humanity was in slavery, trapped by hostile forces, the 'Prince of the Power of the Air', as St Paul put it. Since the coming of Christ however, freedom has been established and announced. This is the declaration of unconditional rescue, which is revelatory and liberational. However this rescue has to be actualised in each individual case by baptism and faith in Christ, so that true transformation comes through participation in Christ, by dying with him in the old age dominated by sin and death, and rising with him to the new age of life and immortality.[8]

---

[8] A useful discussion of Campbell's work is found in Tilling, C., (2014), *Beyond Old and New Perspectives on Paul: Reflections on the Work of Douglas Campbell*, Eugene, Or.: Cascade.

This is a narrative Campbell reads clearly from Romans 5–8, which uses the language of being 'enslaved to sin' (e.g. 6.6, 20), being 'sold into slavery' (7.14), and being 'set free' (6.18, 20, 22; 8.2) from the law of sin and death. It is more problematic in Romans 1–4, which seems, on the surface at least, to tally more with the 'two covenant' models described above, and in which Campbell sees large sections where Paul is quoting an opponent, rather than speaking with his own voice. This, naturally, is one of the more controversial aspects of this reading.[9]

Rather than get embroiled in this rather complex debate, I simply want to draw attention to the significance of Paul's language of freedom and liberation, language that this new 'apocalyptic' reading of Paul has helpfully highlighted. A better text to help us explore this point is perhaps St Paul's letter to the Galatians, in which the theme of freedom is particularly prominent, and in which he faces head-on the kind of opponents he has in mind more explicitly than in the book of Romans.

FREEDOM IN GALATIANS

The Epistle to the Galatians was an urgent letter written by St Paul in around 50 AD to a group of churches he had planted a few years beforehand, probably in some Hellenised Celtic cities of south-central Asia Minor such as Ankyra and Pessinus, in what is now Turkey.[10] In it, he wades straight into a dispute among the Christians of Galatia in which a

---

[9] Those wanting to explore this theme further should look at the chapters by Douglas Campbell and Robin Griffith-Jones (chapters 9 & 10) in Tilling, C., Ed. (2014), ibid.

[10] There is of course an etymological link between the words 'Celt' and 'Galatian', and football fans in particular will connect the name instinctively with the Turkish club Galatasaray, based in Istanbul.

set of teachers related to the church in Jerusalem, claiming that only observance of the Jewish law delivers freedom, have taken over the church, ejecting Paul's own originally appointed catechists and instructors. These are effectively a kind of messianic Jewish group, preaching the law as good news for Gentiles, but insisting that circumcision, the observance of holy times and dietary regulations are necessary for true Christian living.[11]

Much of the letter is taken up with Paul's expression of frustration with the Galatian Christians for allowing themselves to be robbed of their freedom, and enslaved all over again by these Jewish Christians who insist that they submit to the law. Paul will have none of it. Their new-found freedom in Christ is to be jealously guarded, and no-one is to threaten that liberty. For Paul, this submission to the law is not freedom but slavery.

The letter begins with a greeting of grace from 'God our Father and the Lord Jesus Christ, who gave himself for our sins to set us free from the present evil age, according to the will of our God and Father' (Gal. 1.3–4). Right at the start Paul makes this central claim, placed in such a prominent position presumably because it is the heart of the message to which he wants to recall them. Here, it seems, is the centre of Paul's gospel: that Christ has 'set us free from the present evil age'. The Greek word is *exaireō*, which means to 'snatch out of the grasp of', or to 'buy out of enslavement to' something or someone. This formulation compares salvation to the act of manumission – the freeing of a slave. Paul's understanding

---

[11] The reading of Galatians that follows draws particular on Martyn, J. L. (1997), *Galatians*. New Haven, Yale University Press., who favours the more apocalyptic interpretation of Paul.

of the human plight, therefore, is not being guilty of sin in some legal framework, but rather being enslaved to hostile powers. Or as J. Louis Martyn puts it: 'The need of human beings is not so much forgiveness of their sins, as deliverance from malignant powers that hold them in bondage'.[12]

The vital clue to Paul's understanding of the Gospel is perhaps his conversion, when God revealed (the Greek word could be read as 'apocalypsed') Christ to him on the Damascus Road. This was not the discovery of a philosophical idea, or a strenuous breakthrough involving new moral courage, but a dramatic invasion of God into his life. It was not struggled towards, asked for, or even expected. It just happened. This was a truly apocalyptic event for Paul, which made him almost literally a new person, indicated in taking on a new Greek name – Paul – different from his Hebrew name, Saul. This is exactly how St Paul saw the Gospel from then on – as the apocalyptic invasion of God to free those held in slavery, and form a new kind of humanity.

The theological centre of the epistle comes at the start of chapter 4, a passage that bears closer attention:

> My point is this: heirs, as long as they are minors, are no better than slaves, though they are the owners of all the property; but they remain under guardians and trustees until the date set by the father. So with us; while we were minors, we were enslaved to the elemental spirits[13] of the world. But when the fullness of time had come, God sent his Son, born of a woman, born under the law, in order to redeem those who were under the law, so that we might receive adoption as children. (4.1–5)

[12] Ibid., p.273.
[13] A better translation of this phrase might be 'basic elements'.

The metaphor used here is one that was familiar within the first-century Greek and Roman world. It is that of the household, with a master with two kinds of people under his charge – children and slaves. At the time, children, even though they were destined one day to inherit the property, held few rights, and were kept under strict control, discipline and supervision by their 'guardians and trustees' until they reached maturity. Slaves had even fewer rights, having to submit at all times to the orders and whims of their masters, good or bad. It may be that Paul saw the Jews as the children, and Gentiles as the slaves, but in effect both children and slaves were equivalent to each other. As Paul puts it: 'heirs are no better than slaves'.

The image means that humanity, whether Jewish or Gentile, had been held under the power of the 'elemental spirits of the world', or, as it is expressed elsewhere, the 'powers of this present darkness', or perhaps better, 'the basic elements of the world'. (Eph. 6.12). These *stoicheia tou kosmou* probably refer to the four elements of earth, water, fire and air. They are not demonic in themselves, but can be co-opted for evil purposes by demons, leading to enslavement.[14] Pagan worship, as the Old Testament often claimed, was the worship of creation rather than the Creator, and a divided creation at that, with its elemental opposites of air in opposition to earth, fire in opposition to water. Paul seems to have held a fundamental belief, echoed in some contemporary Jewish thought, that the world was held under a

[14] See Tilling, C. (2016), 'Paul, Evil and Justification Debates', in C. Keith & L. T. Stuckenbruck (Eds.), *Evil in Second Temple Judaism and Early Christianity*. Tübingen: Mohr Siebeck. See also Martyn, J. L. (1997), *Galatians*. New Haven, Yale University Press, 394ff and Fung, R. Y. K. (1988), *The Epistle to the Galatians*. Grand Rapids, Eerdmans. pp.189–192 for an alternative view.

kind of spell – the spell of created powers who were hostile to God and humanity, and who used a tactic of divide and rule. Consequently, he is mystified by the Galatians' willingness to be lulled back to slavery from freedom:

> Formerly, when you did not know God, you were enslaved to beings that by nature are not gods. Now, however, that you have come to know God, or rather to be known by God, how can you turn back again to the weak and beggarly elemental spirits [*stoicheia*]? How can you want to be enslaved to them again? (Gal. 4.8–9)

The difference between Paul and these teachers is that they disagree on how freedom is found. The Teachers argued that freedom comes from observance of the law, eating kosher food, being circumcised, and following the Jewish calendar. However, Paul had come to believe that the Jewish law was itself one of the enslaving elements, one of the *stoicheia*, because it perpetuated the ongoing opposition between Jew and Gentile, just as the pagan world continued to be divided hierarchically between slave and free or male and female. The Jewish law, with its distinct demands on Jewish people of different practices, dress and habits of association, was the primary boundary between Jew and Gentile, marking off one from the other, creating a world divided into two. One of the distinguishing marks of the new age of God's liberation was the overcoming of such division. As Paul put it in 3.28: 'There is no longer Jew or Greek, there is no longer slave or free, there is no longer male and female; for all of you are one in Christ Jesus'. The Jewish law was part of the old age that is passing, the age of slavery, and and no longer has any place in the new age of deliverance. It is like one of the tutors who kept the children under strict control while they were minors, and who was no longer needed once the child had matured to adulthood (3.24–25).

But now the time has come when God has invaded this present age through the sending of Christ, 'born of a woman, born under the law', so that the time of cosmic enslavement is past, and the 'slaves' can be freed and adopted as sons. A key word is *exagoradzō*, which occurs in both chapter 3.13 and here in 4.5, is often translated as 'redeem', and usually means to 'buy back' something, or to deliver from slavery. Campbell argues that the language of 'justification' in the letter – *dikaiō* or *dikaiosunē* – actually refers to God's dramatic, liberating intervention in Christ, his act of deliverance, focused on his death and resurrection. Justification happens, or in other words people are set free, not by works of the (Jewish) law, because that is tied up in the old world of a divided humanity, but *pisteōs Iēsou Christou* (2.16). This is a hotly contested phrase, usually translated as 'by faith in Jesus Christ'. However, Martyn, along with an increasing number of other commentators, prefers to translate it as 'the faith of Christ', or even 'the faithfulness of Christ' – what is technically known as a 'subjective genitive'. In other words, people are liberated, or 'justified', by Christ's faithfulness to his purpose, his obedience to the divine plan – through his death on a cross, by which he has brought to an end the old age with all its divisions and brokenness, and ushered in the new age of freedom from these powers – and through the resurrection and ascension, by which he is enthroned as Lord of heaven and earth.

The key question at the heart of the letter is therefore a chronological one: 'What time is it?'[15] Are we living in

---

[15] Martyn, J. L. (1997), *Galatians*. New Haven, Yale University Press, p.104.

the age in which humanity was subject to hostile powers, under slavery to the 'elemental spirits of the world'? Or are we living in the time when God is making all things new, where the war of liberation has commenced, and freedom is proclaimed? If the latter, then this has some clear implications for Christian life.

In chapter 4, Paul continues the imagery of slavery and freedom, climaxing with his stirring call to live in the freedom which is the gift of Christ: 'For freedom Christ has set us free. Stand firm, therefore, and do not submit again to a yoke of slavery' (5.1). The Christian life for these first-century believers is described as a life of freedom. It was freedom for Gentiles, from the degrading demands of pagan worship, where the gods needed to be placated by sacrifices which might just avert disasters inflicted by angry, neglected spirits, or might persuade these capricious deities to organise things in their favour if their sacrifices were impressive enough. It was freedom for Jews, who had been held under the law for a period of time, with all its detailed instructions about food laws, hours and times of worship, and its ethnic boundary markers such as circumcision, into a new law, summed up in a single commandment: 'You shall love your neighbour as yourself' (5.14), or the simple command to 'bear one another's burdens and in this way you will fulfil the law of Christ' (6.2).

This is not just 'freedom from', but 'freedom for'. Back in chapter 4 of Galatians, liberation was depicted as an act of adoption. The newly freed slaves were not simply liberated into nothing, an aimless existence of the 'negative freedom' we looked at before, but were adopted as sons of the family, heirs of the father. They were redeemed from the slavery of the 'basic elements', whether the pagan gods or the Jewish law, to receive 'adoption as children' (4.5), and as Paul continues to say: 'you are no longer a slave but a child, and if a child then also an heir, through God' (4.7). This is a freedom primarily for relationship – with the one who freed them in the first place, and with other freed slaves and children who have entered their maturity. The opposite of slavery for Paul is not autonomy, but relationship.[16]

The coming of the Spirit draws them into the same relationship with the Father as Christ has, so that they cry out to the Father, using not the language of slaves, but the language of sons; in fact it is the same language as used by Jesus the Son: 'Abba Father' (4.6), precisely because by faith they participate in Christ.[17] Paul claims that this new liberty becomes his not by some independent gift, separate from Christ, but through a deep identification with him, and particularly his death and resurrection: 'I have been crucified with Christ', he says (2.19). His life is now an entirely new one, in which the core of his identity is not his previous identity of Saul the learned Pharisee, the persecutor of Christians, but instead, in an extraordinarily intimate and transformational image, 'Christ who lives in me' (2.20). Just as the old age died with the death of Christ, so did the old Saul, and the motivations and desires that shaped his former life: 'those who belong to Christ Jesus have crucified the flesh with its passions and desires' (5.24). They are no

---

[16] The point is made by Bauckham, R. (2002), *God and the Crisis of Freedom: Biblical and Contemporary Perspectives*. Louisville, Westminster John Knox, p.43: 'What the slave lacks is not only freedom from bondage, but also belonging. So when Jesus makes people free, he not only liberates them from bondage to sin; he also makes them children of God his Father.'

[17] For further elaboration of this idea see Tomlin, G. (2011), *The Prodigal Spirit: The Trinity, the Church and the Future of the World*. London, Alpha International, SPTC books.

longer slaves, but sons and daughters by adoption, called into privileged relationship with the one who has bought their freedom.

At the same time, they are drawn into relationship with other recipients of this same gift of freedom. In an unexpected and stunning reversal, Paul calls on the Christians of Galatia to use their freedom by choosing to become slaves again – although not slaves to the 'basic elements of the universe', or the Jewish law, but to each other: 'For you were called to freedom, brothers and sisters; only do not use your freedom as an opportunity for self-indulgence, but through love become slaves to one another'. (5.13).[18] This new law, the law of love,[19] is one that does not divide humanity into two, as the old Jewish law did with Jews and Gentiles, but unites it, creating a new community founded not on ethnic identity, or fragmented devotion to the myriad pagan gods, but on the freedom and unity found in Christ.

This vision is hotly contested, however. The decisive victory was won at the moment when Christ was crucified on a Roman cross outside Jerusalem. The coming of Christ was 'God's invasive act into a space that has temporarily fallen out of God's hands'.[20] Final victory is assured. However, in the meantime, the battle still has to be fought and won, and this battle going on in the Galatian churches is part of this struggle between the new age and the old era,

---

[18] The same language, of freedom dedicated to a freely chosen slavery is used in 1 Cor.9.19: 'For though I am free with respect to all, I have made myself a slave to all, so that I might win more of them.'

[19] Surely this is one of the places where Paul picks up directly on some of the teaching in the Gospels, especially Jesus' teaching on the two chief commandments of love for God and neighbour (Matthew 22.40) and the 'new commandment' of love in John's gospel (John 15.12)

[20] Martyn, J. L. (1997), *Galatians*. New Haven, Yale University Press, p.105.

which refuses to give up control. The sending of the Spirit enlists people as soldiers in that battle, which rages in the contested space of the world where the cosmic powers still claim hegemony, even if in reality their power is broken, and their eventual defeat is guaranteed.

Christ has brought these Galatian Christians into the realm of freedom, but this is no neutral, peaceful space. There is a war going on, a battle between the powers of light and freedom and those devoted to darkness and slavery, even though its ultimate outcome is assured. This battle is not primarily a social and political one, but an apocalyptic war, fought for control of human behaviour. On one side is the Spirit; on the other, the Flesh. The question is, which of these has control? They are not different parts of human existence, the physical and the spiritual elements of human identity, but instead supra-human powers, exercising contrasting gravitational pulls on human action, one of which will always be in control. These Christians have been freed from the 'basic elements of the universe', but cannot stay in a kind of limbo, subject to no-one, suspended in moral and spiritual mid-air. They have to exercise their freedom in one direction or another. Paul raises the possibility that the Galatians might use their new-found freedom from the worship of the gods or the Jewish law to become slaves to their own destructive desires (this is what the concept of 'flesh' seems to mean). Both flesh and Spirit evoke desires (5.17) which are in radical opposition to one another, and the results of choosing to dedicate one's freedom to one or the other of these two powers are clear and very, very different.

Paul gives two lists, which sound like the traditional lists of vices and virtues found in many a Greek or Roman moralist; however, here they are cast into the context of this apocalyptic battle over this small community. It is not so much that they are urged to act virtuously rather than viciously, but that submission to either Flesh or Spirit will result in two very different kinds of community life. Giving in to the desires of the Flesh will result in 'enmities, strife, jealousy, anger, quarrels, dissensions, factions, envy' (5.20–21) – in other words, the very things that will destroy community, and divide humanity all over again. Giving in to the desires of the Spirit will result instead in 'love, joy, peace, patience, kindness, generosity, faithfulness, gentleness, and self-control (5.22), the very things that will build healthy community life.

The key question here is how their new-found freedom is to be exercised: to build or destroy community? The goal in mind here is not some individual existence, freed from the demands of others, liberated into independence, a private space where they can do what they like with their own goods, possessions and property (as in the dream of the libertarian moralists we looked at in chapter two), but rather a form of communal living that will provide the context for flourishing human life. Freedom used simply to indulge the desires of the selfish heart will end up with conceit, competition and envy (5.26), which will destroy any sense of healthy community, and in turn make for deep unhappiness. Paul ends by urging them to 'sow to the Spirit' (6.8), using the imagery of the farmer who carefully sows seed, waiting for it to bear fruit in due time. They are to adopt a pattern of life which invests in practices that will in due time lead to the fruit of the Spirit – a community in which the life of freedom is possible because, paradoxically, each one has chosen to be a slave of the other.

CHRISTIAN FREEDOM

This reading of St Paul, and especially his letter to the Galatians, helps identify the basic outlines of a Christian approach to freedom, which we will see expanded and explored further in later chapters as we trace the way freedom has been conceived in later Christian thought.

First, the idea of freedom has a metaphorical power in the New Testament that it does not have in other contexts, because it refers primarily to freedom from the condition of being a slave. Thinkers such as Locke and Rousseau spent a great deal of time thinking about the 'state of nature', which they imagined as one of freedom and equality, subsequently spoiled by either human competition (Locke) or the corrosive effects of civilisation (Rousseau). St Paul thinks of the 'state of nature' in our fallen state, if we can use that phrase in his context, as not freedom but bondage. Freedom is therefore not a right but a gift. It is not something we deserve, or can create ourselves, but the gift of God, who breaks into the condition of human slavery to bring freedom. There is nothing inevitable about freedom.

Second, the kind of freedom envisaged by Paul is not a blank space, an abstraction, being released into a void. As we have seen, Isaiah Berlin helpfully coined the terms for contrasting negative and positive freedoms – 'freedom from' and 'freedom to'. The former means liberation from the obstacles that might frustrate human choice and action; the latter concerns the question of who or what now directs a person's actions or life. St Paul suggests that the self that is freed from slavery has to learn how to use that freedom, because it will always come under one power or another – the Flesh or the Spirit. The self has to be formed by something; it cannot simply form itself. It is controlled either by the Spirit or the Flesh. It is not alone in the universe, unaffected by anything, purely free to act out of simple naked choice, but is subject to powers that either enslave or liberate.

Third, this liberation is given for the sake of building community. Freedom is granted not to separate individuals from one another or, even worse, to set them against one another, but to bring them into relationship with another. The freedom Paul envisages is not independence, but interdependence. It is not freedom from relationship, but freedom for relationship. Freedom as gift brings a person into relationship with the Giver, and with other fellow recipients of the gift. This is not the freedom that simply gives the sovereign individual a huge range of choices as to how they will spend their time and money. It is emphatically not consumer freedom, valid and valuable though that is. It is instead freedom to create new sets of relationships which come about paradoxically when we learn to become servants of one another.

Richard Bauckham has made the observation that

> instead of replacing a model of society in which there are masters and slaves with a model in which everyone is his or her own master, Jesus and the early church replaced it with a model in which everyone is the slave of others – with of course the understanding that this 'slavery is entirely willing' … If the Old Testament emphasis is on God's people as *freed* slaves, the new Testament emphasis is on God's people as free *slaves*.[21]

---

[21] Bauckham, R. (2002), *God and the Crisis of Freedom: Biblical and Contemporary Perspectives*. Louisville, Westminster. John Knox, p.15.

This captures nicely the distinct view of freedom we find in the New Testament, one that differs both from both ancient and modern views of freedom. In this chapter we have seen some of the foundational building blocks of the Christian understanding of freedom. The next few chapters explore some key Christian thinkers who have developed these ideas, beginning with perhaps the greatest of them all, St Augustine.

6

Freedom Forfeited

Like St Paul, St Augustine of Hippo is one of those thinkers who have shaped the way we think far more than we are aware. With lesser thinkers, you can perhaps try to understand them – get your head around them, so to speak. With great minds, who shape our own thinking from the inside, you can only hope to get a little distance from them, and begin to understand how much they have influenced you. This is pre-eminently true of St Augustine. His responses to the great questions which occupied his mind – What are we made for? How do we associate with one another? What is evil and where has it come from? What exactly does God do for us? What is desire and how does it shape human behaviour? – have deeply impacted the habits of thought of generations of Westerners over the centuries. It is hard to read any thinker before the twentieth century who has not in one way or another been influenced, consciously or unconsciously, by St Augustine.

However, his influence has waned over the past century or more. Flannery O'Connor, with characteristic bluntness, once wrote: 'The Catholic novelist believes that you destroy your freedom by sin; the modern reader believes, I think, that you gain it in that way'.[1] It's a bold way of making the point, but she goes right to the heart of the insight of St Augustine on freedom, and perhaps why the modern secular mindset finds him so hard to understand.

Augustine's view of freedom, like so much else in his theology, is dictated by his lifelong attempt to understand the nature, dimensions and subtleties of love, desire and evil. His biography is really the story of repeated attempts to try to solve the dilemma of the relationships between these forces so central to human experience.

After he left his home in the small provincial town of Thagaste in North Africa for the livelier urban centre of Carthage, Augustine was initially attracted to the mystical, syncretistic, ascetic movement known as Manichaeism. This was an early attempt to arrive at a solution to to the dilemma of the relationship between good and evil, grace and freedom. Recognising the mix of good and evil in the world, the Manichee solution, that good and evil are both eternal, always in conflict, both inevitable and inescapable parts of reality – as it was in the beginning and ever shall be – gave the young seeker a structure of thought which made sense to him and gave him an answer of sorts. Good came from God, and evil was a separate principle, a 'Kingdom of Darkness' that has invaded the world, causing havoc and initiating the eternal struggle between these two equal forces. This dualism existed not just in the world, but in the human soul as well. Human beings are split personalities, a mix of good and evil, and the task of the spiritual devotee was to feed the good side and starve

---

[1] Ellsberg, R. & Giannone, R. 2003, 'Flannery O'Connor: Spiritual Writings', *Modern Spiritual Masters Series*. New York: Orbis, pp.127–8.

the evil, so that one day the soul would struggle free and be liberated.

Augustine tells, however, of his increasing unease with this solution. It seemed to offer a God who was impotent in the face of evil, a God who was hardly worth worshipping. Evil was the vibrant and active force, and goodness seemed somehow passive, quiet and static. Moreover it also seemed to imply that there were two gods – an evil one and a good one. His doubts came to a head when listening to and questioning one of the most celebrated Manichee philosophers, Faustus of Milevis, who was simply unable to answer his growing objections. And so began his slow journey into catholic Christianity, influenced by a potent mixture of Ambrose, Bishop of Milan, a group of Christian friends, and the prayers of his mother Monica.

His *Confessions* returns again and again to this question, reflecting, among other reminiscences, above all on the psychological and spiritual effects of an incident in his adolescence: the theft of some pears. He describes his frame of mind during those teenage years, of having the single desire 'simply to love and to be loved'.[2] He recounts how this youthful hunger led him to drift from God, searching for love and happiness wherever he could find it. When he was 15, during a break from education, as his father's funding had temporarily run out, he was back home in Thagaste, loafing with various friends who, like most bored teenagers in history, began to get into trouble. Very near the family vineyard there was a large pear tree, belonging to a neighbour, and one night they decided to raid the tree, shaking off as many pears as they could before running away.

[2] Augustine (1998b), *Confessions*. Oxford, OUP. II.i.2, p.24.

The adult Augustine is fascinated by this experience. As he recalls it, the desire was not for the pears. They were not particularly attractive either in colour or taste, and Augustine and his friends only actually ended up eating a few, and throwing most of them to the pigs. 'My desire was to enjoy not what I sought by stealing but merely the excitement of thieving and the doing of what was wrong.'[3] Despite recognising the beauty of the fruit, as something God had created, he acknowledges that it was not the fruit that he desired: it was the illicit enjoyment of doing something that was just plain wrong, and the pleasure of doing this with others, finding in this forbidden act a form of connection and fellowship with his friends.

At the end of the reflection, he is struck by the complex and confused nature of evil acts, and how impossible they are to understand. Using an image which becomes a frequent metaphor in dealing with evil, he asks the question: 'Who can untie this extremely twisted and tangled knot?' Yet this very complexity is somehow a key to understanding the problem. As he tries to understand why he committed this act, as he goes through the various possibilities – that he liked the taste of the pears, that he enjoyed the feeling of illicit companionship with others committing this crime together, that he simply enjoyed the pleasure of breaking the law – none of them really answers his question:

> What fruit had I, wretched boy, in these things which I now blush to recall, above all in that theft in which I loved nothing but the theft itself? The theft itself was nothing and for that reason I was the more miserable .... my love

---

[3] Ibid., II.iv. 9, p.29.

in that act was to be associated with the gang in whose company I did it. Does it follow that I loved something other than the theft? No, nothing else in reality because association with the gang is also nothing.[4]

As he tries to understand his motivation, everything just slips through his fingers. Nothing seems to explain it. It is just a mystery. And yet somehow this knotty complexity, this lack of sense in the act, is the clue to understanding what was going on. Nothing can explain it because that is exactly what evil is – nothing. He cannot make sense of evil because it is nonsense. 'To love evil is to love nothing.'[5] As he looks back, he recognises what he was looking for in this simple act of theft. In stealing the pears, what he was really looking for could only be found in God. In fact, all 'sin' is a futile attempt to find happiness and beauty in created things rather than in the Creator. 'The soul fornicates when it is turned away from you and seeks outside you the pure and clear intentions which are not to be found except by return-ing to you.'[6] Here we find the essential movement which lies at the heart of all evil for Augustine: the movement of turn-ing away from God, the source of all beauty and goodness. And if you turn away from God, there is nothing else to turn to. Just nothingness.

This, in essence, is his basic answer to the problem of evil – that it is nothing, or perhaps better, NO-thing: 'Evil has no existence except as a privation of good, down to that level which is altogether without being.'[7] It is not a *thing* at

---

[4] Ibid., II. viii.16, p.33.
[5] Evans, G. R. (1982), *Augustine on Evil*. Cambridge, Cambridge University Press, p.5.
[6] Augustine (1998b), *Confessions*. Oxford, OUP. II. vi. 14, p.32.
[7] Ibid., III.vii.12, p.43.

all, certainly not something which could be counterposed to God as a kind of rival to him, as Manichee dualism had done, because apart from God there is nothing. Evil is not a substance: it is insubstantial, trivial. To commit evil is to turn away from God towards nothingness. Evil is not a positive active principle, a substance or a thing, but a lack of something. It is the absence of good.[8] Augustine also came to believe that to turn away from God towards nothingness was an abuse of original freedom that actually ended in slavery. It is worth spending some time trying to understand how he came to this view.

EVIL, BONDAGE AND FREEDOM

One of his earlier works on this topic was simply called *De Libero Arbitrio* – On Free Will – which comes in the form of a conversation with one of his close friends, Euodius. Here Augustine asks the question of why we do evil in a more formal and less anecdotal way. His answer is that evil arises out of desire for the wrong things. For Augustine, we are shaped fundamentally by what we love. As the philosopher James K.A. Smith puts it: 'Human persons are not primarily or for the most part thinkers, or even believers. Instead human persons are – fundamentally and primordially – lovers'.[9] Our relationship with the world and with God is determined by what we set our hearts on. We are made, not for aimless drifting, but to be oriented towards something, to love something outside ourselves. It is a vision of human life, not as perfectly free to choose its own path, but

---

[8] This is not an original idea to Augustine, nor even to Christianity, but which he found in neo-Platonic thought, even if he developed it in a distinctly Christian direction.
[9] Smith, J. K. A. (2009), *Desiring the Kingdom: Worship, Worldview and Cultural Formation.* Grand Rapids, Baker Academic, p.41.

fundamentally oriented towards the good – a vision we have already seen in the last few chapters through Iris Murdoch, Simone Weil and St Paul.

Originally, this desiring would have been directed simply towards everything that is good, beautiful and true. It would have been ruled by rational considerations, which would recognise truth and beauty for what they were – the most desirable of things. For Augustine, virtue and wisdom are so self-evidently good and attractive, that a purely rational will would always and obviously choose them when it saw them. It would recognise without any doubt that virtue is the route to happiness. If we were entirely rational in our choices, then everyone would choose to act virtuously.

The problem is, as he was to explain so vividly in describing the incident of the pears, that we do not choose virtue, and we do not find God and goodness interesting, attractive or desirable. We do not see goodness and pursue it. Instead, we often devote ourselves to things which are of lesser good, or even things which will ultimately destroy us – which of course raises the question: why? Why do we do what is not good for us? Why do we lash out in anger, burn with jealousy, smoulder in resentment, or get consumed with greed? The blame does not lie in the things we desire in themselves, but the bad use which we make of them. Creation itself is good; it is just that we use it wrongly. There are no evil things – there are just good things used badly or for nefarious purposes.[10] To do evil is to turn away from the source of all goodness, beauty and constancy, and instead

---

[10] 'Every nature is good ... Every substance is either God or comes from God, because every good thing is either God or from God'. Augustine, 1953. 'On Free Will.' in J. H. S. Burleigh (Ed.), *Earlier Writings*: 102–217. London: SCM, p.193.

devote all one's attention to things which are changeable and uncertain. Evil comes therefore from a misuse of freedom. It is to miss the best, to shun beauty, to give oneself to what can never truly satisfy.

There is a complexity to Augustine's understanding of evil here. On the one hand, it is a turning towards created things rather than God. Yet in another sense it is a turning away toward nothingness. How can this be? The answer comes in Augustine's understanding of the purpose of created things: the world was meant to lead us to God, to point us to him. It was never meant as an end in itself, to be enjoyed purely for itself. So, paradoxically, to try to find pleasure and satisfaction purely in physical things and sensations such as fame, sex and wealth, is in effect to turn away from the very thing they are meant to point to: truth, beauty and goodness – which are ultimately found in God. If we try to grasp them for themselves only, they turn to dust and ashes in our hands, crumbling under the pressure of our grip, which is so tight we cannot let go of them, because they are all we have.

Euodius then asks the obvious question: if it was by a misuse of freedom that evil has entered the world, why did God give us the gift in the first place? Augustine's reply is that, just as God has given us hands and feet, even though we can use them for evil, God is right to give us free will even if we end up misusing it. A good action can only be done by someone who is able to choose goodness – a stone falling is not a good action, because the stone can do nothing else. A soul that has the potential to be free, even if it abuses that freedom, is better than one which has no freedom at all. When Euodius goes on to ask the further question – why do people sin? – Augustine answers: 'The will is itself the first cause of sin.[11] And if you ask, why did a person choose to will that specific wrong action? there can be no answer. If you can find a reason behind the will, then it is not an act of the will – it has been caused by something else. We are back with the familiar idea that no reason can be given for sin and evil, precisely because it is irrational. It can have no meaning because it is meaningless.

This was Augustine's answer to the Manichees. They had argued, as many people do today, that because evil undeniably exists, either God created it, or he is powerless to do anything about it, because if he was truly good he surely would. Augustine's answer was that in a sense evil does not exist, in that it is not a created thing at all, but a turning away from God and goodness. It is a misuse of creation, which ultimately ends up destroying that very creation. To ask, 'Who created evil?' was like asking of a broken table, 'Who created the brokenness?' No-one created broken-ness, because brokenness is not a thing: it is a simply lack of something.

THE POWER OF EVIL

This, however, left open the wider question of whether evil had any distinct power, and what, if anything, God did about it. A couple of decades later, when Augustine was an experienced bishop, trying to school his reluctant flock of Christians in Hippo into a love for and desire for God, he began to hear rumours of a British monk in Rome who had taken issue with some of his statements in the *Confessions*. This was Pelagius, a confessor and Spiritual Director who was trying to help some well-heeled Christians in Rome

---

[11] Ibid., p.200.

improve their spiritual lives, and doing so by appealing to their will, telling them they just had to try a little harder. Pelagius saw the human will as being evenly balanced, free to choose good or evil, wrong or right. Whether you progressed in the spiritual life was simply a matter of choice and effort. Pelagius had therefore taken an instant dislike to Augustine's idea that humanity was so damaged by inherited sin that it could do nothing about it. Surely, if evil is 'nothing', then it cannot really do much damage?

Augustine begins to reply to some of these questions in his *De Natura et Gratia* – On Nature and Grace, written in 415 AD. Why, asked Pelagius, if evil is not a substance itself, can it affect the substance of human nature? Augustine replied with a handy metaphor. If we do not eat, then the substance of our bodies is damaged. Food is something substantial, but abstinence from it is not a substance, rather the absence of a substance, with the result that our bodies are weakened, exhausted, and ultimately die. In the same way, sin is not a substance, although God, like food, is. If we withdraw from God, then our whole existence begins to suffer, and we wither away.[12]

For Augustine, all created things exist by participating in God. If they cease to participate in God, the creator and sustainer, they simply cease to exist. As Miles Hollingworth puts it: 'God supports all life and reality in the manner of a vital source, which, if it were for one second to be unplugged, would plunge all of this into instant non-existence'.[13] Therefore to turn away from God

---

[12] Augustine, (1991b), 'On Nature and Grace.' in P. Schaff (Ed.), *St Augustine: Writings Against the Pelagians:* 115–51. Edinburgh: T&T Clark. XX, p.128.

[13] Hollingworth, M. (2013), *Saint Augustine of Hippo: An Intellectual Biography*. London, Bloomsbury, p.93.

is not simply to make a harmless personal religious choice, but to turn away from the source of all life and being itself: it is not freedom, but self-destruction.[14]

Augustine may have successfully solved this problem, but another classic Pelagian question still lurked. Even if you grant that evil, although nothing, can still affect us in deeply damaging ways, all stemming from Adam's original sin, why can we not simply choose to act differently? Surely, if we wanted to, we could choose not to imitate Adam's turning away from God? If the basis of sin is imitating Adam's bad example, the remedy is surely just to try and imitate Christ's good example? Augustine had no problem with the idea that Adam had set a bad example, but believed that the problem was much more intractable. It was as if Adam's sin had meant contracting a disease which had infected every human soul since. He made a vital distinction between actual sin (the daily sins we commit of jealousy, anger, lust, envy, etc.), and original sin – the disease which every human being has carried, ever since the original sin of Adam. The dispute was not over actual sins – both agreed that these happened – but over original sin, and whether there was any inherited ongoing effect of Adam's sin on subsequent generations.

Augustine's observations of the deeply complex and inexplicable nature of sinful action – that, despite the goodness and beauty of truth, we continue time and again to turn away from it towards lesser goods, or even to what will destroy us – convinced him that it was not quite as simple as Pelagius and his supporters thought. There was something more than just imitation going on.

[14] See Bonner, G. (2006), *Freedom and Necessity: St. Augustine's Teaching on Divine Power and Human Freedom*. Washington, D.C., Catholic University of America Press, pp.52–53 for a helpful discussion of this point.

This became a real bone of contention during Augustine's arguments with Julian of Eclanum, sometimes called the *enfant terrible* of Pelagianism. Julian, using rather daring language, argued that 'freedom of choice, by which man is emancipated from God, exists in the possibility of giving way to sin, or of abstaining from sin'.[15] Augustine of course, deeply disliked this language of 'emancipation from God', by which Julian meant that we can turn to God on our own, and don't need God's help to do so. It seemed to diminish God, turning him back into the rather pathetic, powerless deity he had left behind in Manichaeism.

Augustine's problem was to somehow maintain the sense that humans are still responsible for their actions, and yet powerless to change them. His answer was basically that Adam's sin had not only set a bad example which was liable to be imitated by future generations, but had also created habitual behaviour, which inevitably meant that patterns of damaging, destructive sinfulness continued to plague the human race. Writing in 420 AD, Augustine argued that the wicked retained some free will: no-one is forced to sin, but because of the ongoing effects of sin they are only in fact free to sin, because of the force of habit: 'If they are already of the age to use the choice of their own mind, they are both retained in sin by their own will, and by their own will hurried along from sin to sin'.[16]

The result of turning away from the true, the good and the beautiful, argued Augustine, is to lose the very faculty that we are unwilling to make good use of: we lose the gift of freedom. This happened, according to Augustine, when

[15] Ibid., p. 67.
[16] Augustine (1991a), *Against Two Letters of the Pelagians*. Edinburgh, T&T Clark. III.7, p. 379.

the first humans chose to disobey God, turning away from him in the garden of Eden to eat the forbidden fruit. Ever since then humanity had lost the capacity for perfectly free choice, being caught in a web of inherited patterns of behaviour that twisted their desires to look for the good towards creative things rather than God himself. This is not an arbitrary punishment, however. Turning away from God happens because the will simply chooses to find its satisfaction and joy in something else, and this in turn becomes a habit. As Augustine puts it in the *Confessions*: 'The consequence of a distorted will is passion. By servitude to passion, habit is formed, and habit to which there is no resistance becomes necessity'.[17] This explains how, for Augustine, sin leads not to freedom, but to bondage. Adam lost the power to do good because he contracted a kind of moral disability, a twist in his nature, a habit that rendered him no longer able to see and to choose the good. He lost his freedom of choice because he could only choose one thing. Habit became necessity.

For Augustine, evil begins with the inexplicable act of a primeval human decision to turn away from God. It then affects desire, making us think we can be truly happy by seeking satisfaction in such things as food, sex, power, fame and friendship – good things, but never meant to be ultimate goals. This overwhelming desire for such things then clouds our judgement, rendering us unable to think straight, and coming up with all kinds of reasons why these objects of our desire really will bring us satisfaction. It then affects our behaviour, in that we will do anything to get what we have set our hearts upon. This cycle becomes

---

[17] Augustine (1998b), *Confessions*. Oxford, OUP. VIII.v.10, p.140.

an iron chain we are unable to break. Although, of course, Augustine does not use this language, the best example to use is that of addiction. The addict longs for the next fix of the drug. He can be ingenious in convincing himself that the next shot is exactly what he needs and will bring satisfaction and pleasure. And he will do whatever it takes, or whatever it costs, to get hold of the drug. It is no use telling a heroin addict simply to stop. Addiction is a pattern of behaviour much more complex and deeply rooted. For an alcoholic or a drug addict to be clean requires much more radical solutions. Appeals to try a little harder are laughably inadequate. The addict is no longer free to choose to give up the drug; only free to continue in bondage to what will ultimately destroy him.

This is what Augustine means by the bondage of the will. It is not some arbitrary punishment, whereby God takes away humans' freedom in anger at their disobedience. It is the inevitable effect of generations of accumulated, habitual behaviour that turns away from life towards death, from the goodness of being towards nothingness.

In other words, evil, although in one sense 'nothing', does have a sinister power to destroy. Augustine believed that Pelagius simply didn't understand the nature of sin – the act that chooses evil – and evil itself as the impulse towards nothingness, nor did he understand how damaged the human will had been, ever since its original defection from God in primeval history. Pelagius' anthropology was just too simplistic. It could not explain the mysterious persistence of evil behaviour, the outbreaks of selfishness, pride, envy and anger that from time to time take us all by surprise. We think we are free, but in fact we are addicts. Worse still, we are addicts who don't know we are, and who think our drug is harmless, and that we are perfectly free, because we feel that we are. From the inside, the alcoholic feels she is making a free choice as she reaches again for the glass of whisky, releasing herself once again into a relaxed feeling of satisfaction. From the outside, we see it from what it is: an addiction, where she has little choice but to continue in her enslavement to the bottle.

EVIL, DESIRE AND FREEDOM

If sin is the path, not to freedom but to bondage, how, then, is freedom restored? Pelagius argued that if the origins of evil were in an act of the will, surely the answer to evil is in an act of the will – simply choosing to do good rather than evil? Augustine, of course, felt it wasn't that simple. Something greater was needed to break the habit, the addiction to sin. If the taste for God had been lost, something needed to restore it. If the pull of evil was too great, then a stronger attraction needed to be introduced to diminish the taste for evil, and increase the desire for good. Sin has rendered the sinner sick: 'that free will, whereby man corrupted his own self, was sufficient for his passing into sin, but to return to righteousness, he has need of a Physician, since he is out of health; he has need of a Vivifier, because he is dead'.[18] Something has to be done, not just by the human race but for them.

The answer is grace. God gives his grace to us in Jesus Christ, who by the Incarnation illumines our minds, and stirs a desire for God in us again. The union between humanity and divinity in Christ enables our participation in God,

[18] Augustine, (1991b), 'On Nature and Grace', in P. Schaff (Ed.), *St Augustine: Writings Against the Pelagians*: 115–51. Edinburgh: T&T Clark. XXIII, p.129.

the very thing that brings about our freedom to love him and to choose goodness. Through this participation in God comes the gift of grace, and the coming of grace restores freedom. For Augustine, grace comes in two forms: the first is in sacramental form, namely baptism, which releases the baptised from the penalty of 'actual sin' – the ordinary daily sins that we commit that otherwise would attract the judgement of God. It cleanses a person from everything she has done in the past, and applies God's forgiveness, so that the sins no longer stand against her account. Baptism, however, does not remove the desire for sin, the attractiveness of it, the subtle lure of wrongdoing. That has to be achieved by a further kind of grace: 'God heals us, not only that he may blot out the sin which we have committed, but, furthermore, that he may enable us to avoid sinning'.[19] Baptism kick-starts a subsequent ongoing process by which desires are slowly altered, and the baptised begin to lose their taste for everything that would distract them from God and true goodness, and instead find their taste for God growing. In other words, it restores the freedom to choose the good, increasingly empowering the choice of virtue and wisdom, because they are becoming more desirable day by day. This second form of grace gradually frees us to love God and all that is good, enabling us to see evil for the ugly and destructive thing that it is, and God for who he truly is – the source of all true desire, beauty and goodness.

The full meaning of Augustine's doctrine of freedom can be seen perhaps most clearly in a comment right at the end of his magisterial political work, *The City of God,* where he envisages the state of the blessed in heaven, when the two

[19] Ibid., XXVII, p.131.

cities are finally distinguished from one another, and will be 'seen without end, loved without stint, praised without weariness'. His explanation is perhaps a little complex, but worth reading carefully to comprehend what he is saying:

> they will then no longer be able to take delight in sin. This does not mean, however, that they will have no free will. On the contrary, it will be all the more free, because set free from delight in sinning to take a constant delight in not sinning. For when man was created righteous, the first freedom of will that he was given consisted in an ability not to sin, but also in an ability to sin. But this last freedom of will will be greater, in that it will consist in not being able to sin. This, however, will not be a natural possibility, but a gift of God ... God is by nature unable to sin; but he who partakes of God's nature receives the impossibility of sinning only as a gift from God. Moreover, in the divine gift of free will there was to be observed a gradation such that man should first receive a free will by which he was able not to sin, and finally a free will by which he was not able to sin: the former being given to man in a state of probation, and the latter to him in a state of reward. But because human nature sinned when it had the power to sin, it is redeemed by a more abundant gift of grace so that it may be led to that state of freedom in which it cannot sin.[20]

True freedom, the freedom promised to those who progress in their knowledge of and desire for God, is the freedom from

---

[20] Augustine (1998a), *The City of God against the Pagans*. Cambridge, CUP. 22.30, pp.1179–1180.

all that would distract them from gazing on the source of all goodness, beauty and truth – God the creator and author of life. It is freedom from the annoying distraction of all that is less than the best. It is not so much the freedom to be able not to sin (which Adam had in the beginning, but then lost), but a freedom of not even being tempted to sin. It is the freedom of God himself, the one who alone is truly free; freedom precisely not to do what is evil. Freedom for the addict is the freedom precisely not to take the drug; freedom to refuse it; the freedom no longer to desire it. When you are captivated by something wonderful – a spectacular landscape, a piece of music, a child playing, a captivating painting – you want to be able just to gaze at it, give your attention to it wholly, and not be distracted by anything. A fly buzzing around your ears; a phone call asking you about some work problem; traffic noise in the background – all feel like an intrusion. It's not that there's anything wrong with each of them: it's that they have the potential to turn your attention away from what is truly good, to something which is simply trivial.

Augustine's vision is not without its difficulties. There is always in his thought a lingering association of evil with physical matter. Because sin is seen as an inordinate attraction to and love for created things, that can imply that creation is somehow ambivalent, a distraction, and therefore a danger. There is a stubbornly persistent Platonic sense that the spiritual is higher than the physical, a hierarchy of being that Augustine inherited from the very Neo-Platonism that helped him towards his discovery of the idea that evil is nothing. Augustine never quite got over his ambivalence about matter, leaving doubts as to whether he really thought creation was utterly and fundamentally good. Defenders of Augustine would respond that he had no doubt that the creation was good. He inherited both from the Bible and from Neo-Platonic thought the idea that existence itself is a good thing, and that sin is ultimately a denial of existence, a tendency towards destruction, a turning away from being towards non-being. However, this sense of the hierarchy of being which ascends to the beatific vision of God can imply a sense of creation falling away, dropping from view, as the believer looks at God alone, rather than finding God in and through created things.

It also, of course, led to difficulties around predestination. If grace is a gift of God, and there is really nothing we can do about our addicted state, then why does God give grace and freedom to some and not others? This was a point on which Pelagius and his followers pressed Augustine quite hard, driving him near the end of his life towards some fairly uncompromising positions. This is too complex an issue to deal with in any great detail here, except to say that, unlike other theologians who grappled with this issue, he does make a significant distinction between God's fore-knowledge and his deliberate choice as to what will happen in future.[21] Predestination is a puzzle, to be sure, but even without it, free will has its complexities as well, especially when it comes to trying to discern, as Augustine does, why we do what we do. Perhaps, as Augustine suggests, predestination is one of those things that we will only ever understand looking backwards, from the perspective where all things are known. As Miles Hollingworth suggests: 'Predestination might just as well be our chosen word for

---

[21] Those interested in this question will find a useful brief discussion of it in Chadwick, H. (2009), *Augustine of Hippo: A Life*. Oxford, OUP pp.151–157.

the future dream of a science that will leave nothing to chance and all things known.[22]

Augustine's thinking on freedom and necessity have been hugely influential on Western culture. Like St Paul, he had experienced the radical irruption of grace into his life, in a way that he could not attribute to his own effort, but could only be explained by a sovereign act of God. It is at least in part due to Augustine that we have inherited a sense that human life is *for* something. Freedom is not a void, but was always meant to be oriented towards something else. The instinct that we saw in Iris Murdoch, that humanity is necessarily oriented towards the good, is an idea hardly explicable without Augustine's apprehension of the power and beauty of goodness. Where he goes beyond Platonists like Murdoch is his conviction that at the end of the day you can't have the transcendent without God. If transcendence is not personal, but is simply faceless and blank, it can't be necessarily moral. Only when the transcendent and mystical is personal can it also be moral, because morality, in the only form we know it, is a quality of persons.

Augustine's Christian version of the idea that evil is essentially nothing contains a good deal of explanatory power. If evil is nothing, and to commit evil is to turn away from life towards death, then it helps us to see how the choice to turn away from God and goodness towards evil actually diminishes our freedom rather than expands it. Only when freedom is focused on and oriented towards God is it true freedom, because then, and only then, is it freedom to love what is truly worth loving.

[22] Hollingworth, M. (2013), *Saint Augustine of Hippo: An Intellectual Biography*. London, Bloomsbury, p.93.

7

Freedom Gained

Augustine's thought was hugely influential on subsequent Christian reflection on the nature of goodness, evil and freedom. He suggested all kinds of intriguing possibilities and opened up wide vistas of thought, right on the eve of the fall of the Roman Empire and the eclipse of significant theological work over the coming centuries. It wasn't until the revival of learning in the second millennium in Europe that these thoughts were picked up by others, and followed through into deeper engagement with the idea of freedom. It became a major theme for such thinkers as Thomas Aquinas as well as Duns Scotus and William of Ockham, who took very different approaches to the idea of freedom, lines of thought that can help us clarify the contours of a Christian understanding of freedom.

Whenever I speak on the topic of the Christian view of the future, the end of all things, I can easily predict one question that will arise, and it is this: if you believe in some kind of heaven, some final state where we enter into the presence of God, will we be able to sin there? It seems on the surface of it to be an unanswerable question – if the answer is yes, then is it really heaven we are talking about?

If sin is still possible, might it all go wrong, just like it did at the beginning of creation? Yet if the answer is no, then it seems we will have become robots, programmed to do God's will without any choice.

In the last chapter we saw Augustine's answer to this conundrum, his final conclusion to the story of freedom. Human beings, once touched and enticed by grace, will become so enraptured with God that not only will they be able not to sin, they will also be unable to sin. Or to put it slightly differently, in heaven, they will be unable to take delight in sin. They will have free will, so technically could choose to sin, but nobody would want to. The final destiny of humanity is intended as a state of perfect sight and understanding, where our minds, at present clouded and distorted by muddled desires and deceptive manipulation, will be able to see evil and goodness for what they truly are. Goodness will be perceptible as the beautiful and desirable thing it is, and everybody will want it. Evil will appear in its true colours: ugly, deformed, repulsive. People would no more want to do evil than eat their own vomit. This will be a state of true freedom: 'free to give ourselves up to the praise of God ... set free from delight in sinning to take a constant delight in not sinning'.[1]

This notion, that the blessed in heaven will be incapable of sin, which is the definition of true freedom, became the orthodox view in the centuries that followed Augustine's seminal work at the end of the Roman Empire. As Augustine lay dying in Hippo at the end of his life, the Barbarians were literally at the gates, and the Roman Empire was about to

---

[1] Augustine (1998a), *The City of God against the Pagans*. Cambridge, CUP. XXII.30, pp.1178–9.

disintegrate. What followed were centuries of uncertainty, disintegration and the breakdown of the universal Roman culture that held Europe together. During these centuries, theological work in Europe lay at a low ebb, but with the turn of the millennium a new spirit began to animate the brightest minds of the continent. The rediscovery of texts containing Aristotle's philosophy, through contact with Islamic scholars who had preserved them in Arabic translation, gave a new frisson of excitement to the intellectual life of Europe, as a new mood of peace and confidence took hold across the continent. New institutions known as universities began to spring up around teachers of different disciplines in places such as Paris, Salerno, Oxford, Bologna and Cambridge. And with this intellectual renaissance, some of these theological questions began to be explored again. The debate on human and divine freedom was picked up again, and developed in a way that shed further light on the true nature of freedom.

ANSELM ON FREEDOM

Anselm (1033–1109) was an Italian from Aosta, just south of Mont Blanc in the Alps, who had run away to escape his difficult and oppressive father, and eventually found his way, via France, to Britain, to become Archbishop of Canterbury and one of the greatest philosophers of the early Middle Ages. Before that, while Abbot of Bec in Normandy, at some point in the 1080s he wrote a treatise entitled *On Freedom of Choice*, in the form of a dialogue between a student and his teacher. The student starts with the usual questions: if freedom of choice is the ability to choose either good or evil, and we have that choice, why do we have any need for God's help? On the other hand, if we don't have a choice, how can we be held responsible for doing wrong?

Anselm replies by denying the premise that freedom is necessarily the ability to choose good or evil, on the simple grounds that God presumably cannot commit evil, but it would not make sense to say he is anything other than completely free. Like Augustine, Anselm denies that the ability to sin is part of freedom, on the basis that the possibility of losing what you value most is a diminution of freedom, not an enhancement of it:

> Someone who has something good which cannot be lost, is freer than someone who has that thing but can lose it … a will that cannot fall away from the rectitude of not sinning is freer than a will that can abandon that rectitude … The power to sin, which if added to the will diminishes its freedom, and if taken away increases it, is neither freedom nor a part of freedom.[2]

Anselm defines freedom as 'the power to preserve rectitude of will for the sake of rectitude itself'. In other words, it is the power not to lose our basic human orientation towards goodness and virtue, that divine harmony which alone leads to happiness. While we are in danger of losing the attraction towards the good, and instead gaining an attraction to more damaging and sinister things, then that is losing freedom, not gaining it. It is a bit like a person who suddenly gains an insatiable attraction for fatty foods that will ultimately make them obese, and unable to do all the things they once

---

[2] Anselm (2007), 'On Freedom of Choice', in T. Williams (Ed.), *Anselm: Basic Writings*, pp.145–65. Indianapolis: Hackett, pp.147–8.

enjoyed – playing tennis, breathing easily, or playing ener-
getically with their children. Anselm depicts the normal
human experience as being liable to enticement from either
side, and especially, after the fall, the lure of temptation.
When we give in to temptation we are not overcome by it,
but we choose to turn to something we have come to desire
more forcefully. For Anselm, as soon as we turn away from
goodness, we lose our ability to desire it, because that very
desire is a gift of God, which we have now chosen to abandon. We can only retain it if God gives it to us again. The
highest freedom for Anselm is being unable to lose happiness. This is basically very similar to Augustine's position,
although pushing it a little further, with the notion of an
absolute inability to lose the orientation towards goodness.

It is a robust and challenging argument. The idea that
we are more free when our power to choose evil is taken
away from us is certainly counter-intuitive. If there is still
the possibility that I might choose the path of destruction,
then there remains an element of doubt, a nagging potential to fall from what is best for me. The person who is free
from such desire, argues Anselm, is freer than the person
who still experiences the pull of destructive and damaging
desires. This is a twist on the 'freedom from' approach we
saw in earlier chapters. Freedom from the deceitful longings of the heart, or what he calls 'rectitude of the will', is for
Anselm true freedom.

AQUINAS – NECESSARY FREEDOM

The next significant contribution to this debate is the distinct
view of human freedom developed by Thomas Aquinas
(c. 1224–74), who attempts to preserve space for both
human freedom and divine providence. He takes it for

granted that people do have freedom, because without it there would be no morality. Without freedom there is no possibility of moral deliberation, praise and blame, because our actions would be determined from outside: we would not therefore be responsible, and hence cannot be blamed for them.[3] However, he does not see any incompatibility between human freedom of action and divine providence. This providence works in and through human choices, but the immediate cause of each action comes from the person who chooses it. 'It is the will itself that acts, though the change is initiated by God.'[4] God acts on the human will according to its nature, and what happens when God acts on a human will depends on the state of that will: 'He moves the will according to its condition. Therefore, if we should consider the movement of the will regarding the performance of an act, the will is evidently not moved in a necessary way'.[5] It is as if God is a driver who presses his foot on the accelerator, but which direction the car goes in depends on which gear it is in. If it is in a positive gear it will go forwards; if in reverse, it will go backwards.

Aquinas does not believe the human will is entirely neutral. Like Augustine and Anselm, he believes human beings are made for God, and have a natural inclination towards goodness. It is the intellect that is prior to the will, in that the will follows what the intellect presents to it as desirable: we choose to desire what we think is good for us.[6] Freedom is rooted in this natural bias of both intellect and

[3] *De Malo* VI, Aquinas, T. (2003), *On Evil*. Oxford, OUP, p.257.
[4] *De Malo* VI, ibid., p.261.
[5] *De Malo* VI, ibid., p.259.
[6] As we will see later, William of Ockham turned this around, to say that the will is prior to the intellect.

will towards truth, goodness, and the happiness they bring. And that is why God has given us the gift of freedom – that we might desire and find happiness. Aquinas therefore tries to hold together divine action, which gives us the possibility of freedom and initiates our actions, and our liberty to choose our course. God makes us what we are, freely acting agents, places before us the prospect of eternal happiness – what we were made for – and urges us to follow that path. Of course, it is possible for us, in our freedom, to turn away from our proper goal. For Aquinas, we always want happiness, but we do not always want the things that lead to happiness, and may choose to pursue what will ultimately lead to misery. But then, if we do so, we lose the very freedom to find the treasure of happiness for which that gift of freedom was originally given: we have 'lost free choice regarding freedom from moral fault and unhappiness'.[7] To reject God is to act against our nature, to turn away from the purpose for which we were made.

RADICAL FREEDOM

Later in the medieval period, however, we find a very different approach to freedom emerging from either Augustine, Anselm or Aquinas. Duns Scotus (c. 1266–1308) and William of Ockham (1285–1347) are known as voluntarists, because of their radical stress on the freedom of both divine and human wills. Thomas Aquinas believed that our intellects, our rational powers and knowledge could direct our will and desire. Human will follows whatever reason presents to it as the highest good. Scotus and Ockham reverse this. The intellect (whether ours or God's) can show the will

---

[7] Aquinas, T. (2003), *On Evil*. Oxford, OUP. *De Malo* VI, p.264.

what its options are, but the will is free to choose any option – it doesn't have to follow the dictates of reason.

For both Scotus and Ockham, it is vital that God is himself radically free. No-one and nothing can dictate to God what he has to do. God is as he is, and the world is as it is, not because of some prior pattern of goodness or rationality in existence before God and to which God has to conform, but simply because God chose it to be that way. While Anselm, for example, believed that salvation through the Incarnation and Atonement was necessary, as the only way it could happen, Scotus believed it was simply because God chose it to be so. Nothing can dictate God's will: it takes precedence over all reasoning or higher meaning. The sovereignty of the divine will is simply the ultimate reality.

This of course raises the disturbing possibility that God's choices are merely random. If no reason can be given for them, is there any real difference between good and evil? Could God, for example, have freely chosen to be evil rather good? Moreover, how can we be sure that God won't change his mind? This is why philosophers such as Scotus and Ockham distinguished between God's absolute power (*potentia dei absoluta*) and his ordained power (*potentia dei ordinata*).[8] According to his absolute power, God could have created all kinds of different worlds which did not involve inherent contradiction – worlds where grass was blue, where rain was not needed for crops to grow, where gravity did not operate, where Christ did not need to become incarnate. However, out of all of the various hypothetical possibilities, God chose, out of his own radical free will,

[8] See Oberman, H. A. (1963), *The Harvest of Medieval Theology: Gabriel Biel and Late Medieval Nominalism*. Cambridge, Mass., Harvard, pp.30–38 for a useful discussion of this.

to create *this* particular world – according to his 'ordained power'. Having chosen to create this kind of world, he is committed to it and will not change his mind. Thus, the way the world works is predictable. Gravity works and always will – God will not suddenly decide to make things work in a different way so that things fall upwards.

Why this world? We do not know. We cannot tell, and it is useless even to speculate. Out of all the ways we could have been saved, God chose the particular way through Christ. There is nothing inherently essential or necessary about the created order, or about the order of salvation, but they emerge out of the supremacy of the divine will, which can have no prior determining factor. Having decided to create this world, and to save humanity through the life, death and resurrection of Jesus Christ, and through the appropriate human response to this, God is now committed to acting this way. This led to a new emphasis upon God's covenantal commitments. In his freedom, God has limited his options and is now committed to this world and to a particular way of salvation. This involves God making a freely chosen covenant with humanity, to reward them with the gift of grace if they turn to him, and to withhold his grace if they turn away.[9] This distinction between the two powers of God was a useful and neat way of showing how God can act reliably, but not out of necessity, as though he were forced to. It helped demonstrate how God is free, but not arbitrary.[10]

---

[9] Martin Luther was schooled within late medieval nominalism, particularly the form adopted by Gabriel Biel, but eventually reacted against this particular soteriological move.

[10] See McGrath, A. E. (1987), *The Intellectual Origins of the European Reformation.* Blackwell, Oxford, p.75.

When it comes to human choice, Aquinas (along with Augustine) had argued that God had placed within human hearts the desire for happiness – a bias in that direction – and freedom to pursue it, even if that freedom had been damaged through the fall and the effect of sin. Scotus and Ockham, however, argued for the human will being perfectly balanced and 'free' from such divine manipulation. For Scotus, the human will does not have to choose at all, as it is perfectly free to choose either. On the question of freedom in heaven, Scotus is so convinced of the inviolable freedom of the will, that in his opinion it is possible, in principle, to choose sin even there.[11] The blessed are able to sin, even in heaven, because they have free will. However, God in his providence has decreed that they will not have the opportunity to use this power, because the higher freedom of the blessed in infinity must involve the inability to sin. He prevents them from sinning by deciding to preserve them in the act of enjoying the vision of God, so that they never actually exercise their ability to sin.

For William of Ockham, freedom of choice is paramount. The human will is radically free, and dictated to by nothing and no-one. As with the divine will, you cannot get behind human free choice to anything prior that dictates or forces it. This is a doctrine that presumes the entire freedom of the individual to choose. It is not determined by any external reality to which it has to conform. For Ockham, freedom is absolutely primary: it is the power to choose – yes or no. The human will is not conditioned, as it was for Augustine and Aquinas, by its attraction towards the good, originally

---

[11] See Gaine, S. (2003), *Will There Be Free Will in Heaven?: Freedom, Impeccability and Beatitude.* London, Continuum, chapter 4.

created as oriented toward God and goodness. It is alone in its lofty freedom.

Ockham is well known for his denial of 'Universals'. These are unifying essences that similar things share. So, for example, we know there are many individual trees, but a believer in 'universals' would argue that each individual tree is an instance of the universal concept of 'tree' or 'treeness', which exists metaphysically beyond the material world. For Ockham, 'such a universal is nothing other than a content of the mind, and therefore no substance outside the mind and no accident outside the mind is such a universal'.[12] Universals are simply conventional signs, a convenient way of speaking about various things that have a number of features in common. Universals are just 'names', a philosophical position that gave rise to the concept of 'Nominalism', of which Ockham is one of the major proponents. This idea again had its uses – it was an attempt to free God from the idea that he was bound by some pre-existing essence of things, some prior form of rationality to which he had to conform. It was a radical statement of the absolute freedom of God, which, as we will see in later chapters, is a vital part of the story of a Christian understanding of freedom.

Consequently, for Ockham there is little point in speculating on what might have been in the *potentia dei absoluta*, and the kind of exploratory questioning that fills Thomas Aquinas' *Summa Theologiae* is just a waste of time. Hence the famous Ockham's Razor – the principle that the simplest explanation is the best, resulting in the desire to eliminate as much unnecessary argument or speculation from

[12] Boehner, P. (1990), *Ockham: Philosophical Writings*. Indianapolis: Hackett, p.34.

philosophy as possible. This of course also limits the extent to which rational enquiry can really make sense of God or the world. It is why many have felt since that Nominalism gave up on rationality, order, and any link between faith and reason, which have to operate simply in mutually independent spheres, the first related to the things of God, the second for the study of nature. It is why some have traced the supposed conflict between science and religion to this movement of medieval thought.[13]

It also explains why some have felt that Nominalism inevitably leads towards human autonomy from God, and is the beginning of a drift towards secularism in Western culture.[14] The human will is so autonomous and free, that it is independent of the divine will. If there are no universals, then there is no such thing as 'humanity', just individual human beings, left radically free to choose their own way. When it comes to the question of whether the righteous can sin in heaven, Ockham ultimately says they cannot, and do not really have freedom in heaven. If he were to concede that the blessed in paradise are truly free, then he would have to admit that they would be free to sin, and therefore to fall all over again. We are entirely free to choose, unless God causes us to will in a particular direction, which is what happens in heaven, and the will cannot do anything else. God as it were ultimately and eventually overrides our freedom, if we co-operate with him along the way.

---

[13] See the fascinating discussion in Chesterton, G. K. (1986), *Saint Thomas Aquinas, Saint Francis of Assisi*. San Francisco, Ignatius Press, opposing Aquinas' thought to that of Siger of Brabant, who advocated a similar split between reason and faith in the C13th.
[14] See Milbank, J. (1990), *Theology and Social Theory: Beyond Secular Reason*. Oxford, Blackwell.

TWO KINDS OF FREEDOM

Behind this debate lie two basic kinds of freedom. In a very illuminating discussion of medieval thought, Simon Gaine describes these as 'Freedom of Indifference' and 'Freedom for Excellence'.[15] Ockham was the main instigator of 'Freedom of Indifference', which has become the primary notion of freedom envisaged in Western culture today, and that we have already seen in Locke, Rousseau and Mill. Freedom is an absolute value. The will is seen not as naturally made for good, but as merely indifferent, closely guarding its independence, because any inclination towards anything outside itself would feel like an encroachment on its own precious freedom. This is freedom indifferent to any prede-termined direction, inclination or external determinism, any sense that freedom might be constrained by another. It is exercised as obedience to external commandments and precepts, the will freely choosing to follow whatever it thinks best. With this kind of freedom, loyalty to something else becomes a threat, because it ties you to something other than your own naked self. For William of Ockham, freedom is found in the autonomous self, and morality becomes a battle between freedom and external laws which might be necessary for social harmony, but which at the end of the day constrain and limit it. The 'other' becomes a threat to my freedom, exactly as we saw in the later libertarian tradi-tion of Locke, Rousseau and Mill.

'Freedom for Excellence', however, sees morality not so much as obedience to laws, as following the inbuilt desire of

---

[15] Gaine, S. (2003), *Will There Be Free Will in Heaven?: Freedom, Impeccability and Beatitude*. London, Continuum, p.88. Gaine acknowledges that he borrows the idea and the terminology from Servais Pinckaers OP, but the subsequent discussion is Gaine's own.

the heart for what is good and true. It is the freedom to be able to do precisely what we were made to do – the things that will bring us the happiness we desire, but which otherwise would be impossible.

Gaine offers the analogy of learning to play the piano. Imagine two sisters. One loves the sound of beautiful music, and so decides to learn to play the piano as well as she possibly can. She starts to learn her scales, gets a teacher, and practises daily. The other sister is fairly indifferent to music, and decides to do nothing, to retain her freedom from the repetitive chore of daily piano practice that her sister seems chained to. Eventually, the first child acquires the ability to play the tunes she loved as she was growing up. She gains the 'freedom', if you like, to play this beautiful music, a freedom which the other sister, in her carefully guarded indifference, does not. Gaine describes this new kind of freedom as 'the gradually acquired ability to execute works of desire with perfection'.[16] Another example is the ability to speak a new language. An Englishman moves to Berlin, but finds himself limited by his inability to converse with his neighbours and work colleagues because he speaks German very badly. Drawn by the desire to join in conversations fluently, and to understand what instructions he is being given at work more clearly, he sets himself to learn, taking evening classes, giving up his social life to attend lessons, spending hours learning German vocabulary and grammar. Gradually he acquires the facility, the freedom to speak easily and naturally with his German friends. To begin with, he keeps making mistakes – grammatical errors, or simply forgetting his vocabulary. He feels frustrated at

[16] Ibid., p.94.

his inability to make sense of what is being said to him, or to communicate his own thoughts and feelings. He seems bound to make errors in his spoken German, condemned to misunderstand what is being said to him. However, over time he gains the freedom not to make mistakes as he speaks German. The capacity to make errors, or to break the rules of German grammar, is not really freedom at all, but a form of bondage, or incapacity; an inability to flourish and fly in the new language. This is true freedom – not the blank cheque, the naked potentiality to choose any option, but the ability to do something well, which comes from limiting one's options by committing to a certain course of action and not turning back.

Freedom of indifference, the kind Ockham wanted to preserve, always wants the freedom to pursue or to reject happiness if it chooses to. That is why we struggle when we ask the question of whether there can be freedom in heaven. If we think, as we habitually do in the West, of freedom as an infinite range of choices, as the ability to choose entirely freely with my sovereign will, then of course heaven is an infringement of that freedom, because it closes the door to one particular option – to choose to turn away from God, from life, from goodness. Ockham tries to avoid this by eventually denying freedom in heaven at all, and asserting a divine *fiat* as the cause of an inability to sin. Scotus also reduces freedom in heaven to a remote power which is never in fact actualised. Both have God intervening to impose a solution, ultimately imposing his will on us, and infringing our freedom.

Freedom for excellence, however, the freedom to devote ourselves to what we are made for, to our ultimate goal, is precisely the kind of freedom we yearn for, and can expect to find in heaven. This kind of freedom necessarily rules out actions or choices that would take us away from our ultimate goal. However, that is only a problem if we are wedded to 'freedom of indifference'. Freedom for excellence is the freedom to become all that we were meant to be. It is the freedom to pursue God, the one in whom we will find our true happiness, free from any distractions, inhibitions or hindrances that would stop us reaching that goal. In the language of the Epistle to the Hebrews, it is the freedom to 'lay aside every weight and the sin that clings so closely, and ... run with perseverance the race that is set before us' (Heb. 12.1).

Imagine a football match, a tight fixture between two rival and evenly matched teams. The crowd is gathered around the sides of the stadium, intently watching the action. They are of course free to spend the afternoon looking up at the sky, watching the clouds drift by, but no-one does. They are transfixed by the action in front of them. Technically speaking they have the freedom to do something other than watch the match, but the attraction of the game captivates them so that it becomes impossible to keep their eyes off it for a minute. In a similar way Aquinas, following Augustine, suggests that in heaven eternal happiness cannot be lost. The reason is that, when a person sees God clearly, that vision is so attractive, so full of wisdom and beauty, that no-one who truly sees him could or would turn away: 'it is only those who are willing who are shown him. But once they have looked, they can no longer turn away'.[17]

Aquinas' view of freedom – freedom to act in accord with our true nature, to be our true selves – is freedom that has a direction, a purpose. Of course, we use this kind of language today all the time – I need to be able and free to 'be myself'. The difference is that we tend to use it in an entirely self-deterministic way. This again is one of the outcomes of the individualising move made by Ockham and others. If I am entirely free as an individual; if there is no universal concept of human nature to which I have to conform, nothing that exists prior to my own naked freedom to choose, then I am free to construct my own identity as I wish – I can be myself, but that 'self' is decided and created entirely by me, and no-one can tell me what to do or to be. We end up with one of the staples of modern self-help motivation: the idea that I can simply define myself, and no-one can gainsay that self-definition. Augustine and Aquinas' view of freedom, however, is that it is determined by what we were made for. Our identity and purpose are given by the one who made us – God, and the pattern of humanity we see in Jesus Christ – and although that longing is spoiled and twisted by sin, it remains our fundamental created inclination, waiting to be restored by grace.

The voluntarist tradition of Duns Scotus and William of Ockham is another attempt to seize freedom, and protect it at all costs, but in the process it risks losing it all together. Like the libertarian tradition of more modern times, of which it is a precursor and ancestor, it is an attempt to grasp the ungraspable, to try and save one's life. But as Jesus paradoxically teaches, it is by losing our life that we save it. Moreover, it is by giving up our vaunted freedom of indifference, our sovereign autonomous will, in order to pursue goodness and truth, that we find true freedom – the freedom to be what we were meant to be, the freedom to be our true selves in God.

8

Freedom and Bondage

Not long after these medieval discussions on freedom, another debate broke out in European intellectual life, this time not over the kind of the freedom people possessed, but over the extent of that freedom in relation to God and to ordinary social life. It is a discussion that illuminates our theme because it probes more deeply into what we might call a psychology of freedom – how freedom works in human motivation, and the extent to which we really are free from all the influences that swirl around us; a discussion that recalls the more contemporary questions about freedom we looked at back in chapter three.

In 1517, Martin Luther had unwittingly launched what became the Protestant Reformation by his publication of 95 *Theses on the Abuse of Indulgences,* supposedly posted on the door of the Castle Church in Wittenberg.[1] The following years saw a series of tense and increasingly charged exchanges with representatives of the Papal church, all

---

[1] At least so the story goes. Luther only ever said he wrote a letter to his Archbishop. The nailing story came later from his friend Philipp Melanchthon. See Iserloh, E. (1968), *The Theses Were Not Posted.* London, Geoffrey Chapman.

trying to argue this truculent German monk into submission. None of them succeeded. In fact, each one drove Luther to express himself in more and more extreme ways. In 1520, with his name now famous (or notorious) across Europe, and the prospect of excommunication looming on the horizon, he wrote three treatises that in many ways were the defining documents of the Lutheran Reformation. The first, 'On the Babylonian Captivity of the Church', was a stinging critique of the stranglehold that the Papacy had put around the European church. The second, 'To the Nobility of the German Nation', was an appeal to the lay leaders of Germany to rise up and reform the church, if the clerics were not going to do it. The third, the most famous and effective of them all, was entitled 'On the Freedom of a Christian'. It was to be one of the most widely read expositions of Christian liberty ever written.

At the time, Luther was in the eye of the storm. His other writings of this period are full of furious accusation, defence and argumentation. Strangely, at this moment of gathering clouds and impending doom, this piece is a pool of tranquillity, an eirenic piece of writing that breathes peace, delight and security. He was so pleased with it that he claimed it 'contains the whole Christian life in a brief form, provided you grasp its meaning'.[2]

CHRISTIAN FREEDOM

The work starts with a bold statement that neatly encapsulates the paradox of freedom:

[2] Luther, M. (1960–90), *Luther's Works*. Philadelphia, Fortress Press. (henceforth LW), 31.343.

A Christian is a perfectly free lord of all, subject to none.

A Christian is a perfectly dutiful servant of all, subject to all.[3]

To explain what he means by this, Luther makes a distinction, crucial to his argument, between the outer and the inner person. It is often misunderstood. Luther does not have in mind a dialectic between some kind of inner self and a person's outward physical appearance – a Platonic dualism of body and soul. Rather, the distinction is a relational one: the 'inner man' is the person as oriented towards and relating to God, and the 'outer man' is the person oriented towards and relating to other people. The 'outer man' is therefore human life seen in social terms. In relation to God, each individual stands alone, unable to rest on anyone else's merits or faith. However, in society we are inevitably social beings, drawn from the very outset into relationship. Luther is often seen as one of the architects of modern individualism, but this is only true in relation to God, not others in society.

The 'inner man', the part of human life oriented to God, is nourished by the word of God, which assures him of God's love, grace and favour, a message which can only be responded to by a faith which trusts that the promise can be relied on. This faith is a truly powerful thing for Luther. It renders human religious or even humanitarian works redundant in establishing this relation to God; it honours God because it ascribes to him the worship and trust he is due; and it unites us with Christ in a unity as close if not closer than between a bridegroom and a bride.

[3] LW 31.344.

The Christian is not an insignificant figure, burdened and restricted by sinfulness and an inferior status which severely limits his options and freedom to think and to act, but truly a king, exercising authority over all things, with all the freedom such a status brings, and, moreover, a priest with rights of access to the very presence of God himself. Freedom for Luther, therefore, exists primarily in this realm, the realm of the 'inner man', in relation to God. It is very definitely an inner freedom, the freedom from fear or anxiety that anything can ultimately harm the Christian who trusts God. It is the freedom from sin and its power, the freedom to be and to do good. This of course does not mean that such a person is free of trials. In fact, 'The more Christian a man is, the more evil, sufferings and deaths he must endure, as we see in Christ ... and the Saints'.[4] However external, such things cannot affect his inner freedom, his relationship to God, due to the strict distinction Luther draws between these two worlds. In this inner realm, there is the freedom of a clear conscience and a restful heart; freedom from any human rules, demands and burdens laid on the sensitive conscience.

This is the most fundamental and basic form of Christian freedom. It is ultimately, for Luther, the only freedom that counts, because it is freedom before God himself. The question then comes: how is this freedom to be used or exercised? This is when he turns to the 'outer man'. The person thus freed from sin, anxiety and fear devotes his freedom to serve the other, not because he has to, but because he delights to do so:

[4] LW 31.354.

From faith thus flow forth love and joy in the Lord, and from love a joyful, willing and free mind that serves one's neighbour willingly and takes no account of gratitude or ingratitude, of praise or blame, of gain or loss. For a man does not serve that he may put men under obligations. He does not distinguish between friends and enemies or anticipate their thankfulness or unthankfulness, but he most freely and most willingly spends himself and all that he has, whether he wastes all on the thankless or whether he gains a reward.[5]

This voluntary chosen service is not balanced against freedom, as though it were a kind of necessary compensation in case we think ourselves too free: it is an expression of freedom. It remains free because it is freely chosen, not compelled. If love and service were somehow necessary for salvation, they would become a burden, imposed from outside, not freely chosen but basically offered because we have to. Moreover, they become acts which are not truly acts of love. If a person's motive in an act of generosity is not ultimately to bless the other person through the gift, but really to gain personal merit, to win their own salvation, or, as we might put it in our own day, to look good, then it is not really an act of generosity at all. Only if the act is performed entirely freely, without need for any personal reward, does it become a genuine act of love and willing service.

The distinction between inner and outer is strict, but it is not the case that they have nothing to do with each other. Inner freedom has implications for outer life. Precisely because of this inner freedom, the Christian freely chooses to

---

[5] LW 31.367.

become the servant of others. Having received this freedom as a gift from God, she gives her freedom as a gift to others. The outer self requires the exercise of certain disciplines so that the outer body conforms to the prior and more basic inner reality of freedom. If the body is not ordered and disciplined, it falls out of line with the inner reality, and fails to reflect it:

> In this life he must control his own body and have dealings with men. Here the works begin; here a man cannot enjoy leisure; here he must indeed take care to discipline his body by fastings, watchings, labours, and other reasonable discipline and to subject it to the Spirit so that it will obey and conform to the inner man and faith and not revolt against faith and hinder the inner man, as it is the nature of the body to do if it is not held in check.[6]

All the time, Luther is keen to stress that disciplines, actions or works do not in themselves bring about freedom. Only the Word of God, received by faith, does that. In the context of late medieval Christianity, a great deal of resources, effort and religious activity were put into ensuring personal salvation. Pilgrimages, indulgences, masses for the dead all sucked up vast amounts of money and time. Luther's radical claim that such things achieved nothing in the realm of salvation suddenly released all that energy, time and money to be used to serve the poor and the neighbour. As Brian Gerrish put it: 'the liberation of a man from constant anxiety about the condition of his soul is what makes him available to his neighbour'.[7]

[6] LW 31.358–359.
[7] Gerrish, B. A. (1982), *The Old Protestantism and the New: Essays on the Reformation Heritage*. Edinburgh, T. & T. Clark, p.89.

Two points can be made about Luther's vision of freedom. The first is that, for Luther, freedom is sheer gift. It is grace. It does not come about as a result of reward for services rendered to God, or as a right demanded from him: it is a gift which gives inner liberty, regardless of outward circumstances.

The second point is that because this freedom is a gift, it creates relationship. The Christian, free of the fear of sin, guilt, death and all the hosts of Satan, chooses to dedicate her freedom not to self-indulgence and to pleasure, but to the neighbour, because this freedom has been given as a gift. The gift creates a sense of gratitude and a kind of free obligation, a freely chosen service. This gratitude then issues in a renewed use of this freedom, exercised communally, not individually, as we saw it was for St Paul in chapter five. Whereas other visions of freedom, such as those we explored in the libertarian tradition in chapter two, separate us from others in a privileged space of private liberty, making the 'other' a potential enemy who threatens my freedom, this vision of freedom creates relationship, in that this inner freedom is actively expressed in service of others. There is for Luther a direct link between inner freedom and the outer use of that freedom as given to other people, and the link is the concept of freedom as a gift. As Luther says: 'I will give myself as a Christ to my neighbour, just as Christ offered himself for me'.[8] There is a correlation between the free gift of freedom from Christ, and the free gift of service to the neighbour. A Christian lives, not in himself, but 'in Christ through his neighbour through love'.[9]

[8] LW 31.367.
[9] LW 31.371.

These are the broad outlines of Luther's view of Christian freedom: freedom as gift, given by God and received by faith alone, which then, by virtue of its sheer gratuitousness, evokes a corresponding giving-up of freedom, to become the 'perfectly dutiful servant of all'.

FREEDOM AND BONDAGE

This was a positive, attractive vision of freedom. However, it also had its negative, polemical side. As Gerhard Ebeling put it: 'no theologian – we may even go further and say no other thinker – has spoken in such compelling terms of the freedom of man on the one hand, and with such terrifying force of the bondage of man on the other'.[10] Back in 1518, when he had appeared at a theological disputation in the University of Heidelberg, Luther had written: 'Free will after the fall, exists in name only, and as long as it does what it is able to do, it commits a mortal sin'. This was one of Luther's most controversial early statements, which was in turn picked up and condemned by the Papal bull which threatened him with excommunication, and which reached him in October 1520, just over a month after he had published 'The Freedom of a Christian'. For Luther, if the human will was active, trying to contribute something to salvation, then by definition it cannot receive it as a gift. In fact, we commit sin by actively trying to earn something which was meant to be given as a gift. Luther had insisted from early on in his break from medieval soteriology that when it comes to salvation, we contribute nothing. Even faith is not a 'thing', an action we perform: it is merely the

[10] Ebeling, G. (1972), *Luther: An Introduction to His Thought*. London, Collins, p.211.

passive trust that holds onto the promise of God that offers justification, forgiveness and freedom.

In 1525 this negative aspect of his view of freedom took a more controversial and polemical turn. By now, Luther's break from the Roman church had taken place, and he was already set on a trajectory towards establishing a new form of church life. Before long, his idea of freedom came into conflict with one of the few comparably famous figures in European intellectual life, Desiderius Erasmus.

Luther and Erasmus had a good deal in common. They had both been educated in the movement known as the Brethren of the Common Life; both were well-known reformers who denied the value of Aristotle's influence on medieval theology, disliked the Scholastic method and opposed the practice of indulgences. Both valued the Bible, and the study of its original languages, and advocated the reform of the church by the laity. Their early exchanges had been friendly and mutually admiring. However, as Luther's own language became more extreme after his break with the papacy, Erasmus grew increasingly uneasy with the younger reformer. Erasmus, the cool, detached Renaissance man, began to be annoyed by the fiery Teutonic passion of Luther's rhetoric.

Erasmus also disliked the dim view Luther took of human abilities and powers. He thought Luther's insistence that humankind could do nothing to contribute to its salvation, and could only believe in the promise of God extended to it, was demeaning to the dignity of humanity, something sacrosanct to a Renaissance humanist like Erasmus.

Provoked into taking on Luther by none other than Pope Adrian himself, as well as by the growing rumour that, as he had not written against Luther, he must be his supporter, in September 1524 Erasmus published *De Libero Arbitrio,* A Discourse on Free Will, directly attacking Luther's idea that justification comes by 'faith alone', and what he considered Luther's dogmatic and aggressive tone, particularly on the issue of the human will.[11]

An obvious corollary of Luther's idea of freedom as free gift, to be received by faith, was the idea that without faith, there is no freedom. In fact, for Luther, free will is a fiction. Erasmus wanted to claim some space for human action, arguing that if humans were not capable of responding to God's commands, then, on the one hand, salvation would seem arbitrary, and, on the other, an important plank of morality would crumble. If there is no free will, who will ever make any moral effort at all? Who will reform their life? For Erasmus, the message that we are simply bound, with no wriggle room at all, no capacity to do anything in response to God, is a recipe for moral laziness. At the same time, Erasmus simply wanted Luther to calm down. His was never a dogmatic position (he was, after all, never a dogmatic person). He only wanted Luther to tone down his rhetoric and admit some small space for human action, especially as this was not a cardinal issue of faith, and was not very clear in the Scriptures anyway.

Luther replied just over a year later with characteristic confrontational directness, entitling his response *De Servo Arbitrio*: On the Bondage of the Will. The writing veers between respectful disagreement, withering critique and robust polemic. Its terminology is not always very exact,

---

[11] He had originally wanted to write a dialogue between a Lutheran, his opponent and an arbitrator, a casual, ruminatory discussion which would have been more calm, but probably a format unsuited for the heated nature of the debate that became necessary.

and sometimes downright confusing,[12] but the main outline is clear.

The same distinction between inner and outer man we saw in his earlier 'Freedom of a Christian' remained implicit behind the discussion. With regard to 'outer' things – life in society – there is a degree of freedom. This is the realm of 'things below us', ordinary life decisions such as what to have for breakfast or what clothes to wear. In this realm, there is genuine though limited freedom to choose and to act. In the realm of 'things above us', the inner man, the realm of our relationship to God, however, there is no freedom of the will at all. And this is no 'obscure doctrine' as Erasmus suggested – it went to the heart of the gospel:

> I praise and commend you highly for this also, that unlike all the rest you alone have attacked the real issue, the essence of the matter in dispute, and have not wearied me with irrelevancies about the papacy, purgatory, indulgences, and such like trifles (for trifles they are rather than basic issues), with which almost everyone hitherto has gone hunting for me without success. You and you alone have seen the question on which everything hinges, and have aimed at the vital spot.[13]

This was life and death. Everything hinged upon it. Luther pulled no punches: 'Here, then, is something fundamentally necessary and salutary for a Christian, to know that God foreknows nothing contingently, but that he foresees

---

[12] Paul Hinlicky writes of the 'shoddy imprecision of Luther's terminology': Hinlicky, P. R. (2010), *Luther and the Beloved Community: A Path for Christian Theology After Christendom*. Grand Rapids, Eerdmans, p.156.
[13] LW 33.294.

and purposes and does all things by his immutable, eternal, and infallible will'.[14] Here we hit upon one of the most rigorous arguments for the absence of human freedom since Augustine's work over a millennium beforehand.

Why then does Luther see this as such a vital issue? Luther builds up a number of arguments which contribute to the same aim: to undermine any confidence in human independence from God which he sees as the basis of free will.

First, he argues that free will is something only properly ascribed to God. God alone is free to choose without any restriction on his choice, with nothing external to him which influences his choice. That much he had learnt from his Nominalist tutors in Erfurt, who followed William of Ockham on this point. However, this has a consequence when it comes to human choice. Breaking from his Nominalist education, he claimed that the inevitable corollary of this was that humans have no free will with regard to God. At the end of the day, either God or we have free will – we cannot both have it. If we did, they would come into conflict, and that is logically impossible. God's choice to save us, for example, would come into conflict with our desire not to be saved. Either God obeys and does what we want him to, or we obey and do what God wants us to – you can't have both. There cannot be two free wills.[15]

Second, building on this point, Luther argues that God's will must prevail, otherwise God's promises cannot entirely be trusted. For Luther, salvation rests wholly on the promise of God. As he put it in 'The Freedom of a Christian':

[14] LW 33.37.
[15] See Jenson, R. (1994). *An Ontology of Freedom in the* De Servo Arbitrio *of Luther.* Modern Theology 10(3): 247–252.

'The promises of God give what the commandments of God demand and fulfil what the law prescribes so that all things may be God's alone, both the commandments and the fulfilling of the commandments'.[16] God gives his grace and goodness to us as a gift in Christ, and the appropriate response to a gift is simply to accept it. The appropriate response to a promise is just to believe it. Moreover, if God's promise is to be fulfilled, the only way we can be sure of it is if there is absolutely no question that it can be honoured. In other words, if some events are outside God's control, then that leads to doubt as to whether his promise will ultimately be kept:

> For if you doubt or disdain to know that God fore-knows all things, not contingently, but necessarily and immutably, how can you believe his promises and place a sure trust and reliance on them? For when he promises anything, you ought to be certain that he knows and is able and willing to perform what he promises; otherwise, you will regard him as neither truthful nor faithful, and that is impiety and a denial of the Most High God. But how will you be certain and sure unless you know that he knows and wills and will do what he promises, certainly, infallibly, immutably, and necessarily?[17]

For Luther, only necessity preserves the trustworthiness of the promise of God.

Third, any concession to human free will brings salvation into doubt. If salvation rests even just a little on human

[16] LW 31.349.
[17] LW 33.42.

activity – some slight human action, as Erasmus wants to claim it must – then this too brings salvation into doubt. Questions inevitably arise. Am I capable of what is being asked of me? Have I done enough for salvation? Is my contribution what is required? This is exactly the kind of fear that Luther had been delivered from in his original break from the soteriology of his contemporaries in the theological world of late medieval Christianity, and it is easy to see why he did not want to go back to that spiritually debilitating uncertainty.

Fourth, and here we come closer to the nub of Luther's argument, introducing human free will into the relationship between God and humankind paradoxically limits our freedom rather than establishing it. Erasmus had argued from morality, that unless there is some human freedom to obey God's commands, no-one would bother to make any moral effort. The problem with this, as Luther delights to point out, is that Erasmus actually becomes the theologian of the law, envisaging a heteronomous law set in opposition to the human will. Our supposed human freedom to choose thus comes up against a barrier, a command that tells it what to do. It finds itself opposed, restricted, confined by the law. The human will is no longer free to do as it wants, but is ordered to obey against its true inner desires. In this dynamic, the hidden, secret pull of sin, whether gossip, envy, pride or lust, has to be sublimated and suppressed, but never quite dealt with. Luther, on the other hand, sees no need for the law in the realm of salvation, thus envisaging the Christian soul as free from the law and its demands. The will is only set free by the word of God, which declares it forgiven, pardoned, justified. Paradoxically, by emphasising human free will, Erasmus ends up as the theologian of bondage, and Luther, by emphasising bondage, ends up as the theologian of freedom![18]

Luther's conviction is that free will is actually a fiction. It is a chimera, a fantasy that doesn't really exist. Why does he say such an apparently outrageous thing? Luther is reacting against the kind of thinking on freedom we saw in the last chapter, associated with philosophers like William of Ockham.[19] Their idea of 'free will' implies a perfectly balanced will, free from any external influence whatsoever. In what became a famous image, Luther depicts the human will as like a horse that is ridden by one rider or another – either God or the devil.[20] The two riders fight for control, and the way the horse faces is determined by which rider has the reins. Luther's contention is that our wills are not entirely free to choose, as Ockham thought they were. We are at the play of forces outside ourselves. We deceive ourselves that we are in charge, but this is a fiction. We say we do what we want, but that is exactly the problem – we are bound to do what we want, and what we think we want is swayed by things other than our own will. As it says in the New Testament, 'people are slaves to whatever masters them'. (2 Pet. 2.19).

For Luther, only God has the kind of will that is entirely free of external influences. Human wills cannot just choose to change themselves – we cannot choose what to choose. And what we choose is not ultimately under our control.

---

[18] See Forde, G. O. (2005), *The Captivation of the Will: Luther vs. Erasmus on Freedom and Bondage*. Grand Rapids, Eerdmans, chapter 2.

[19] Luther's early intellectual training was in the nominalist school of philosophy current in the University of Erfurt, under his tutors Joducus Trutvetter and Bartholomäus Arnoldi von Usingen. For the best study of late medieval Nominalism, see Oberman, H. A. (1963), *The Harvest of Medieval Theology: Gabriel Biel and Late Medieval Nominalism*. Cambridge, Mass., Harvard.

[20] LW 33.66.

If you are suddenly overtaken with an urgent desire for chocolate ice cream, to go swimming, or to tell a lie to get out of trouble, you cannot simply choose to 'turn off' that desire. You can try and suppress it, but then you are effectively curbing your freedom to act according to your wishes, which, Luther always points out, is a kind of hypocrisy, doing one thing while secretly desiring and thinking another. We are unable to change our desires, as they are fundamental, and those desires are pulled one way or the other by forces external to the self. As Paul Hinlicky puts it: 'there is no freedom of desire; the will, taken as desire, spontaneously and necessarily seeks what appears good to it and flees what appears evil. This capacity is what Luther has in mind when he denies that the will can move itself; that is, cause itself to desire something'.[21] To change the metaphor, free will is like a car in neutral gear, unable to do anything. It only moves when a driver puts it into one gear or another, at which point it is no longer neutral – it is fully engaged, either to go forward or reverse.

To use another image, Erasmus' idea of free will seemed to imagine a moment on the scale between willing God's will and not willing it, where the will is perfectly balanced and free, leaning neither to the one nor the other. The problem Luther sees with this is that the will is always drawn one way or the other, like a finely balanced see-saw which leans one way and, when it swings upwards and reaches the tipping point, then automatically leans over toward the other side. There is no neutral moment when it is perfectly balanced horizontally: it either leans one way or the other.

---

[21] Hinlicky, P. R. (2010), *Luther and the Beloved Community: A Path for Christian Theology After Christendom*. Grand Rapids, Eerdmans, p.157.

The idea that the human will is free – in other words, perfectly balanced and free to choose its own course of action, completely independent of any external influence – is a fantasy. As Geshard Ebeling says: 'The will is always already decided, involved and committed, and is not the natural will in the situation of absolute freedom of choice, the will considered in purely unhistorical terms. The will is only the free will to the extent that it is able to do what it wishes.'[22] As we saw in chapter three, the idea that we act uninfluenced by external factors is an illusion; our decisions are always swayed by desires, moods, arguments, persuasions and enticements from outside, that determine what we think we choose far more than we realise.

This is a basic difference of anthropology from Ockham. Ockham thinks the will is primary and can shape our desires. Luther thinks it is psychological and theological nonsense. His is a more Augustinian anthropology that says desire comes before will. Our desires shape our thinking, not the other way round. And if God is the Creator who created us for himself, then we are either drawn to him as we were created to be, or running away from him to try to establish our own freedom, which is no freedom at all, because it leaves us captive to any old whim that takes over our pliable and easily-led hearts.

CAPTIVATED INTO FREEDOM

Luther's writing is usually bold and brash. His doctrine of freedom is one of the more stark and dramatic statements of the paradox of freedom. It starts with a conviction that

---

[22] Ebeling, G. (1972), *Luther: An Introduction to His Thought*. London, Collins, p.220.

freedom is not a right that can be demanded, nor something deserved or earned – in fact, such doctrines of freedom tend to set up a gap between desire and action, giving no good reason for acts of goodness or building social life, leaving the soul isolated in their freedom, with no reason, other than a reluctant obedience to heteronomous law, to create social bonds. Freedom instead is a gift that creates rather than destroys relationship: first, a free relationship of trust with the God who is the giver of freedom, because the gift is received precisely by faith, the bond that unites us to Christ the giver of freedom: 'faith ... unites the soul with Christ as a bride is united with her bridegroom. By this mystery, as the Apostle teaches, Christ and the soul become one flesh'.[23] It then creates a social bond with others, in that it frees the sinner from anxiety about his own salvation and releases him for relationship with those around him in acts motivated by genuine love for the other, not for a selfish desire for personal salvation: 'A man does not live for himself alone in this mortal body to work for it alone, but he lives also for all men on earth; rather, he lives only for others and not for himself'.[24]

It has to be said that this argument perhaps works better in the context of sixteenth-century Europe, where anxiety about salvation was a common experience. However, there are some important themes here for our broader discussion about freedom.

For Luther, the bondage of the will is not mere determinism, as it is for the Swiss Reformer Huldrych Zwingli, and in some versions of later Calvinism. It is more like an addiction, in that we do what we are bound to do: 'We all do what

[23] LW 31.351.
[24] LW 31.364.

we want to do! That is precisely our bondage'.[25] This is, as it is in Augustine, the freedom of the addict to take a drug. No-one forces her to; she is not made to by some external law, but she takes it anyway. She feels free to do as she chooses, but in reality we know she has no choice. Put more positively, we might imagine being in love. We do not coolly sit down and choose what or whom to love; instead we are captivated by the vision of someone or something, and that love then dictates our actions. As Luther puts it: 'the will cannot change itself and turn in a different direction ... Ask experience how impossible it is to persuade people who have set their heart on anything. If they yield, they yield to force or to the greater attraction of something else; they never yield freely'.[26] This is not some psychological erasure of the will, imagining human beings as robots, or automata who just do what they are programmed to do. There is an element of willing, but the will follows the pull of a powerful attraction. As Heinrich Bornkamm put it, Luther 'does not mean psychological compulsion but posits the necessity of a higher order that guides the will from above, no matter spontaneously it may act'.[27]

The *Libero Arbitrio* that Erasmus had in mind seemed to envisage a perfectly balanced will, free to choose its own object of love. Luther's point is that this is theologically and anthropologically untrue – it is observably false from human experience, as much as it does not accord with Christian theology. This is why Luther roots the bondage

[25] See Forde, G. O. (2005), *The Captivation of the Will: Luther vs. Erasmus on Freedom and Bondage*. Grand Rapids, Eerdmans, p.37
[26] LW 33.64–65.
[27] Bornkamm, H. (1983), *Luther in Mid-Career*. London, DLT, p.450. See chapter 16 for a detailed and extended discussion of this debate.

of the will not so much in a post-lapsarian state, as in our created nature: this is a basic disagreement on anthropology. Humans are loving creatures. We act when we are captivated by something outside ourselves. The big question is: what captivates us? God? Or something, or someone else? The entry of sin into the picture just complicates it. If there were no sin, we would still be enraptured, but only by God. The fact of sinfulness opens up the possibility of being enraptured by something pernicious, by the objects of our own selfish desire, or even by Satan himself. If our vision and desire are not captivated by God and goodness, they get captivated by something more sinister. As Gerhard Forde puts it: 'unless the Spirit of God enters into the matter, the will goes badly'.[28]

In Christ, the divine Word that proclaims God's nature as gracious and kind, we find something that truly captivates us. This Word gives us a God we can love, and a God that captivates us into freedom, so to speak. Robert Jenson asks the obvious question: why are we delivered into freedom when God captivates us, and not when we are captivated by Satan, or by anyone else for that matter? The answer is that it is because God is the only One who is truly free, in the sense that he is not subject to any external force: his will is not determined by anything outside himself; he is entirely in control of his own will and desire for himself, within the love that exists between Father, Son and Holy Spirit. So, when God enraptures us, we are enraptured into his freedom. When Satan or anyone else captivates us, they cannot draw us into freedom because they don't possess it themselves.

---

[28] Forde, G. O. (2005), *The Captivation of the Will: Luther vs. Erasmus on Freedom and Bondage*. Grand Rapids, Eerdmans, p.55.

Only God can give us freedom, because he is the only one who possesses it. He is enraptured by nothing external, but only by himself, in the trinitarian logic of the Father and Son enraptured in love in the Spirit. 'Human freedom in the only sense Luther wants to talk about, is nothing less than participation in God's own triune rapture of freedom.'[29]

God's freedom, as Luther suggested when he expounded the Freedom of the Christian in 1520, is the freedom to give ourselves to each other in love, not because we have to, compelled by some external law, not because we are pre-programmed to, but because we are freed to do so, released from the self-serving requirement (in medieval terms) to acquire personal merit for salvation, or (in our terms) to impress others, prove ourselves, or establish our sense of self-worth and goodness by doing good things. This is the freedom of what Hinlicky calls the Holy Spirit-inspired 'ecstatic selfhood of faith',[30] the self that is liberated from self-interest and obsession, and thus free for the neighbour. Building on Luther's insights, though put a little differently to how Luther would express it, a Christian vision of freedom imagines people released from the pull of destructive desires, not to leave them stranded with an arbitrary free will, perfectly poised and free to choose either good or evil (as Erasmus had suggested), but captivated by a vision of a good, kind and gracious God who draws them into relationships of love, interdependence and delight, which are exactly the kind of relationships we find at the heart of God himself.

---

[29] Jenson, R. 1994, 'An Ontology of Freedom in the *De Servo Arbitrio* of Luther', *Modern Theology*, 10:3, 247–52.

[30] Hinlicky, P. R. (2010), *Luther and the Beloved Community: A Path for Christian Theology After Christendom*. Grand Rapids, Eerdmans, p.169.

We have reached the end of our discussion of Christian ideas of freedom. In these past few chapters, we have sketched the idea of freedom developed in St Paul, Augustine, Aquinas and Luther, which, although they have their shades of difference, have enough in common to depict a distinct view of freedom. This is not naked freedom, liberty to choose exactly what we want, but a freedom determined by our fundamental orientation as human beings towards God and goodness. We are not perfectly balanced free beings, but were always meant to be aligned towards God, even though that basic alignment has been complicated and twisted out of line by sin, like a compass whose orientation to true north is skewed by another magnet placed too near it. As a result, we are torn, pulled one way or the other, not in control of our own willing or desire but at the mercy of forces beyond ourselves, more so than we ever think. These early Christian thinkers put this in terms of being pulled between God and Satan. As we saw in chapter three, in our modern world, we can see that we are seduced and directed more than we know by clever marketing, technology, peer pressure or networks of power in which we are caught. The answer found in these Christian theologians is grace: the restoration of our original longing for God who alone can make us truly happy and free. This grace delivers us into a form of freedom which is not freedom from the demands of others, but freedom to give ourselves in service to others, thus creating rather than destroying community life.

In the final two chapters of this excursion into freedom, we draw the argument together with a glance at one of the strongest ideas underpinning our notions of freedom – human rights – and then a final chapter explaining the paradox of freedom.

9

A Right to Freedom?

Over the past four chapters, starting with St Paul, and tracing the story through Augustine, Aquinas and Luther, we have uncovered a Christian account of freedom that is very different from the libertarian vision that has become dominant in the modern world. It would be a mistake to see this purely as a Christian-versus-secular argument, however. As we saw, some Christian voices, such as William of Ockham or Duns Scotus, painted a quite different portrait of freedom, and the vision we traced in the Augustinian Christian tradition finds an echo in the atheist Iris Murdoch as well as the rather unorthodoxly Christian Simone Weil.

The libertarian tradition sees freedom as liberation from restrictions. There are of course different versions of this. The political right tends to see it as freedom from economic restraints that inhibit the free operation of the market, arguing for lower taxation, removal of economic regulation and trade barriers, and giving people the freedom to work, trade or invest. The political left tends to see it as liberation from past social and moral restrictions, the slavery of social, racial or gender expectations which restrict free individuals from realising their inner selves and prospering in their own self-chosen and self-defined way. Both versions dream of the individual being able to expand his or her own domain, while at the same time duly observing the limits of others' needs, along the lines outlined by John Stuart Mill in his principle of never encroaching on another person's freedom unless the intent is to cause harm to other people. The individual must be free to pursue his or her own interests, as long as they do not interfere with the rights of others to do the same.

The difficulty with all of this, as we saw earlier, is that this doctrine leads inevitably to a competitive state which pits the interests of individuals over against each other. This leads on the one hand to envy, as we watch one another compete in the race for success, prosperity or fame, and on the other, imagining 'other people' as an inherent threat to the expansion of our own territory. They become a potential inhibition, marking the boundary of my freedom, and they must, if my ambition to expand is strong, be in some way overcome. Despite its claim to social harmony, this is a vision that is actually a recipe for competition, envy and hostility – exactly what we see so often in modern developed societies.

FREEDOM AND RIGHTS

One prominent way in which the dream of freedom in the modern world is expressed is in the language of rights. 'We have a right to be free' is an almost unchallenged statement, and the desire for free expression and self-determination is routinely and powerfully articulated using the language of rights. The idea of freedom lies at the heart of the UN Declaration of Human Rights, first issued in 1948. In the Preamble's seven brief clauses the word appears no fewer than six times, as the Declaration looks forward to 'the advent of a world in which human beings shall enjoy freedom of speech and belief and freedom from fear and want'. In fact, in several places in the Declaration 'rights' and 'freedoms' are used interchangeably, as in 'everyone is entitled to all the rights and freedoms set forth in this Declaration'. In our modern mindset freedom and rights are intertwined: freedom is seen as a natural human right. When it was drawn up, the UN Declaration was a response to the specific and fundamental transgression of human dignity in Nazi Germany and during the Second World War. However, what was originally a limited and protective set of protocols to prevent atrocity and abuse, and to give practical effect to ideas of basic social freedoms, has since become, as we shall see, an overarching meta-narrative that governs so much of our thinking about behaviour and society. Is this the best way to think of freedom – as a right to be claimed?

Human rights have a contested history. Lynn Hunt's book *Inventing Human Rights* traces the idea's origin to the Enlightenment in the eighteenth century, and particularly to the rise of individualism.[1] Some time between 1689 and 1776, she claims, rights that were assumed to be the possession of freeborn men began to be ascribed to all people. The phrase 'human rights' appears first in 1763 in French, as *'les droits de l'homme'*, and during the course of that decade became a popular and commonly used phrase, even though it is hard to find an authoritative definition from that time of what those rights were. Human rights as thus envisaged depended on the assumption that human beings

[1] Hunt, L. (2007), *Inventing Human Rights: A History*. New York, W.W. Norton.

were individuals with their own inner life or interior feeling. Hunt links this to the rise of the epistolary novel in the eighteenth century – works as Samuel Richardson's *Pamela*, or *Clarissa* – or stories like Daniel Defoe's *Robinson Crusoe* of individuals imposing their will upon an inert world. All these novels display the growing awareness that individuals have inner feelings, self-possession and independence: 'Underpinning these notions of liberty and rights was a set of assumptions about individual autonomy. To have human rights, people had to be perceived as separate individuals, who were capable of exercising independent moral judgement.'[2]

Hunt continues the story of human rights with, from the 1770s onwards, the gradual outlawing of torture – paradoxically, the guillotine was introduced as a compassionate mechanism to deliver a quick and humane end, rather than the prolonged suffering meted out through torture. The individual became more solitary, silently appreciating art in the theatre or gallery, taking walks in carefully laid-out gardens, or, as the Romantic poets did, in the wilds of nature. 1789, of course, saw the French Revolution, and the 'Declaration of the Rights of Man and Citizens'. This proclaimed that rights flow not from a contract between the ruler and the ruled, but from the very nature of human beings as free individuals who have inherent rights.

From now on, governments were to be justified by their adherence to and observation of universal human rights. At this stage in history, two different kinds of rights were envisaged: one was rights due to particular groups – so, for example, the emerging independent America gave rights

[2] Ibid., p.27.

to all men who owned property, regardless of religion or origin, but denied them to women, blacks or the propertyless. At the same time, a second conception of rights began to emerge, in the language of universal human rights – rights that were universal in scope, such as Locke's idea of the rights of Life, Liberty and Estate. Gradually, different groups claimed and obtained these universal rights. As an extension of the French Revolution, rights were extended to Protestants in 1787, blacks (as they were called at the time) in 1792 and slaves in 1794. In Britain, Roman Catholics won the right to serve in the armed forces, study in universities, gained access to the judicial system in 1793 and from 1829 could enter Parliament. Jews were granted the same electoral rights in 1845. Even so, before the end of the nineteenth century women were allowed to vote almost nowhere.[3]

Hunt then describes a hiatus in human rights discourse lasting through the nineteenth century right up until the UN Declaration of Human Rights in 1948. This was due partly to the rise of the 'Terror' in France, with Napoleon restoring slavery to the French colonies in 1802, but also to the rise of nationalism in the nineteenth century, when the language of rights focused not on universal human rights but on the self-determination of nations. Human rights depended on the presumption that human beings were essentially all the same, and when the overriding cultural emphasis in the early decades of the twentieth century was on what made nations and races different, such universal language was bound to fade into the background.

---

[3] The one exception is New Zealand, where women first voted in 1893.

Samuel Moyn, perhaps the most prominent revisionist historian and commentator on the rise of human rights, tells the story differently.[4] While acknowledging the contribution of the revolutions of the eighteenth century, he thinks the human rights proclaimed then were very different from the ones we tend to invoke today. The approach taken by Hunt and other human rights enthusiasts tends to ignore the historical specificity of the idea, and the way in which, as Moyn puts it, 'formal invocations of rights can sometimes mask narrow agendas'.[5] The French Revolution did not in fact give rise to an international human rights movement, and Moyn dates the significant rise of 'human rights' language not to the 1770s, or even the 1940s, but the 1970s. Before then, it had predominantly been used as a slogan for the creation of new emancipated nations emerging from the colonial past, or for freedom from exploitation. It was commonly used as a cipher for freedom from state control. Before the 1940s, 'rights' language deriving from the Enlightenment and the French Revolution was mainly about the rights of nations and national sovereignty. Only after the UN Declaration of Human Rights in 1948 did it focus on the rights of individuals over the state.

However, even after this date, the language of human rights remained peripheral. No-one could define authoritatively what it meant, and consequently the term remained a fairly meaningless slogan. In the 1930s, it had been used primarily in Christian, mainly Roman Catholic, thinking,

---

[4] Moyn, S. (2010), *The Last Utopia: Human Rights in History*. Cambridge, Mass., Belknap. Moyn's reaction to and review of Hunt's book is found in Moyn, S. (2014), *Human Rights and the Uses of History*. London, Verso., 1–17.

[5] Moyn, S. (2014), *Human Rights and the Uses of History*. London, Verso, p.11.

with writers such as Jacques Maritain developing the idea of the human person, rather than the individual, standing between collective anonymity and unencumbered individual freedom, as the object and recipient of human rights. The Roman Catholic church at the time frequently used the language of rights as a bulwark against the overbearing state represented by the rise of atheistic communism.

Human rights remained peripheral before the 1970s, Moyn suggests, partly because they were usually linked to anti-communist movements, especially among Catholics in Europe, and as a result were not able to transcend or solve the left–right divide that dominated politics during the 1940s and 1950s. During this period they had the feel of a bourgeois idea that could never quite gain widespread agreement. Whatever the reason, human rights played a relatively small part in the project of European post-war rebuilding.

The anti-colonial and civil rights movements of the 1950s and 1960s, meanwhile, were more interested in the self-determination of groups or nations than in universal human rights. Malcolm X and the black emancipation movement in the USA, for example, used the language of *civil* rights, not *human* rights. For Moyn, it is the 1970s that mark the breakthrough of human rights as we know them today. After the imperialist threat had diminished and Cold War interventionism, represented above all by the debacle of the Vietnam war, was seen to be a failure, human rights could emerge as the new principle shaping the foreign policy of nations like the USA. They were invoked in backing dissidents like Aleksander Solzhenitsyn and Andrei Sakharov in the Soviet Union, whose freedom agenda meant not the state's freedom from colonial powers, but the individual's freedom from the state. It was President Jimmy Carter who first set human rights at the centre of his foreign policy rhetoric, making a point of meeting dissidents, and assisting individuals to resist repressive regimes.

It was only after the 1970s that human rights began to inform international law as a major factor in shaping legislation. They became a moral agenda, transcending politics, and supplanting communism, fascism, revolution and other utopian visions which had all aimed to change the world for good.

Samuel Moyn's account envisages two future trajectories for the human rights movement. It becomes either a minimalist means of preventing abuse, or a new politics to shape a new world. He is pessimistic, however. None of the other twentieth-century utopian visions were able to deliver a new, fairer and more habitable world, so is there any reason to think human rights can succeed where others failed? Lynn Hunt's account is more hopeful, but also cannot help ending on a downbeat note, recognising the inability of the United Nations to enforce its own declaration and halt the resurgence of national, racial and religious violence across the world. Why has the idea of human rights been unable to stop the various genocides that seem to have become more, not less common in the twentieth and twenty-first centuries? And is there a limit to the interest groups that can claim their own rights? To what extent do such rights extend to children, animals or criminals, for example?

The history of human rights is important, because if, as is often thought, freedom of expression, action or thought is conceived as a right, then that concept of 'rights' needs to be robust and clear enough to support it. Does the history of human rights suggest this as the best way to think of freedom?

THE CHALLENGE TO HUMAN RIGHTS

Despite its popularity, the notion of human rights and, in particular, the grounding of freedom in human rights, face a number of challenges in the modern world.[6] Four main ones can be identified.

THE GROUNDS OF RIGHTS

The first problem arises when we ask about the basis on which human rights are established. Immanuel Kant argued that human rights were granted to those who had rational agency. The UN Declaration of Human Rights grants them on the basis that human beings are 'endowed with reason and conscience'. On the other hand, the International Covenant on Civil and Political Rights, issued in 1966, bases its appeal on 'the inherent dignity of the human person', and the International Convention on the Elimination of All Forms of Racial Discrimination from 1965 grounds rights in 'the dignity and equality inherent in all human beings'.

Of course, most human rights talk emerged from the Western political and philosophical tradition, which many non-Western cultures would not recognise unreservedly. For example, the frequent disagreement between Western nations and China over human rights comes from the ancient Chinese Confucian emphasis on close personal and familial relationships, rather than the autonomous individual as the fundamental building block of society. As Charles Taylor asks: 'Can people who imbibe the full Western human rights ethos, which reaches its highest expression in the lone courageous individual fighting against all the force of

---

[6] For this section, see Posner, E. (2014), *The Twilight of Human Rights Law*. Oxford, OUP.

social conformity for her rights, ever be good members of a "Confucian" society?[7]

Furthermore, there is a difficulty in finding any grounding for human rights in some kind of innate human capacity. Basing 'rights' on rational capacity, as the original UN declaration does, by seeming to privilege rational capacities, jeopardises the entitlement of those whose rational faculties are diminished, such as those with special needs or disabilities. It also leaves it unclear whether children, for example, are included within these rights, and at what age they can be deemed to have them. After all, we do not generally grant children the right to vote or buy land.

The more sophisticated the capacity (such as rational ability or the ownership of property, as in some earlier doctrines of rights), the more likely are certain groups of people, such as the disabled, or migrants, to be excluded. The less sophisticated the grounds (such as basic consciousness, or merely 'being alive'), the more these rights potentially extend beyond humans to animals and other forms of life, and so become meaningless as 'human' rights. The question comes down to how we define humanness, and whether there is any coherent way of finding a particular internal capacity which all humans possess that could serve as a solid basis for human rights.

THE SPECIFICITY OF RIGHTS

This leads onto a further difficulty: that of actually making human rights into a programme that can be enacted. The

---

[7] Taylor, C. 2011, 'Conditions of an Unforced Consensus on Human Rights', *Dilemma and Connections*: 105–23. Cambridge Mass.: Harvard, p.109. The chapter is a fascinating exploration of cultural difference in the field of human rights language.

problem arises when it comes to interpretation. Rights can end up meaning whatever we want them to mean. In the post-war world, for example, after the 1948 UN Declaration of Human Rights, the USA interpreted them as meaning the political rights to vote, to exercise freedom of speech, to practise religion, etc. The Soviet Union, on the other hand, saw them as guaranteeing economic rights – the right to work, to be educated, to receive free health care and so on. When countries can interpret rights as they choose, and when rights are described in such vague terms, they carry little weight. When Vladimir Putin, the Russian President, can cite the rights of ethnic minorities in Ukraine to justify military intervention there, and China uses 'the right to development' to favour economic development over political liberalisation, one suspects the rhetoric of rights has become co-opted to enable a government simply to do what it wants. The numerous treaties were top-down attempts to impose a morality upon the international community that enshrine some vital principles of justice, but, due to the lack of legal sanction and the vagueness of their expression, are virtually unenforceable. And we haven't even got to the question of who is to enforce such rights, especially when the dispute crosses national borders, without the existence of an effective international body to protect, define or enforce rights, even if we wanted such an ominous institution to exist!

When it comes to a 'right to freedom', the same problems surface. What does it actually mean in practice? Does a Muslim jihadist have the right or freedom to defend the integrity of his religion by shooting those who mock and lampoon it? Does an atheist have the freedom to ridicule Christianity, suggesting that it is a damaging and pernicious influence on society and should be eliminated? Does a Christian fundamentalist have the freedom to defend the rights of the unborn by attacking abortion clinics? That such actions can be defended by the use of the language of freedom and rights illustrates the problem. when the language of rights applies indiscriminately to almost everyone and everything, can it mean anything much?

Samuel Moyn puts his finger on the problem. 'Like all universalist projects, human rights are violated every time they are interpreted and transformed into a specific program. Because they promise everything to everyone, they can end up meaning everything to everyone.'[8] In his article 'Against Human Rights', John Milbank makes a similar point.[9] Milbank sees modern subjective rights as rooted in Ockham's Nominalism. The Nominalist scheme, as we saw in chapter seven, sees the individual as a free entity, self-sufficient in his own sovereignty, which stands before any subsequent relationship with others that might limit that freedom. Milbank, however, sees the person as 'constituted through all the relationships in which he stands. It is the unending series of relationships tending towards relationship with God himself which ensure the essential place of the individual within the whole'.[10]

The difficulty comes, he claims, when individual rights are projected onto the whole of humanity. It then proves difficult to work out who to claim these rights from. Is it God? This is a conclusion disallowed by an avowedly secular liberal state. Or is it the rest of humanity itself that is to

[8] Moyn, S. (2014), *Human Rights and the Uses of History*. London, Verso, p. 86.
[9] Milbank, J. 2009. 'Against Human Rights.' http://www.theologyphilosophycentre.co.uk/papers/Milbank_AgainstHumanRights.pdf
[10] Ibid., pp.19–20.

guarantee these rights? And how is humanity to guarantee the rights of every single person to a first-class education, sufficient holidays, excellent and limitless healthcare, or to buy a house? Milbank concludes:

> So this notion of human rights clearly provides us with no practical ethical guidance. In reality it leads to a state of anarchy which is only ended by an authoritarian power which will arbitrarily promote one set of rights over another – liberal states the right of property; State socialist authorities the rights to food, health, work and culture. The former will be at the expense of majority economic well-being; the latter at the expense of people's rights of free association and free choosing of roles and an order of existential priorities.[11]

If human rights are to be granted by the rest of humanity, that basically means the state. If the guarantor of rights is the government, then that leads to greater regulatory power, and intervention by government to ensure such rights are upheld. That, however, sets up a very difficult paradox, even an antinomy: to ensure the preservation of rights, stronger state power is required, and an ever tighter set of rules to tell citizens what they can and cannot do to ensure they do not infringe on each other's rights. But a stronger and more interventionist state is itself a threat to individual freedom, and leads to good deal of suspicion of 'big government': it undermines the very thing it is designed to preserve. It is a very hard circle to square, and the contradiction lies at the heart of a lot of our modern

---

[11] Ibid., p.26.

political debates. We are back with the vision of Hobbes and Locke, or even Rousseau's General Will, with all the difficulties we saw back in chapter two.

THE EFFECTS OF RIGHTS

The language of rights has also been criticised for cultivating an adversarial culture in social life. Asserting my own rights can be a legitimate claim for dignity and value, yet at the same time can become a way of asserting myself over against others. In standing on my right to do as I choose, to say what I choose, to exercise my freedom, this so easily becomes a way of asserting my right not to be interfered with by you. You have no right to trample on my rights. The 'other' again becomes a threat to my rights, not a gift to be welcomed. My right to freedom is my right over yours, in case you try to inhibit my freedom.

The libertarian view of freedom we have explored in this book is based on an individualist anthropology, which Milbank traces back to William of Ockham and the Nominalist turn of the fourteenth century. If we are first and foremost individuals, defined by our subjective autonomy before our relationships with God or with anyone else, then that plays into a doctrine of human rights, but it is a doctrine of rights that, like the libertarian view of freedom, pits individuals against one another, or against the state which is meant to guarantee those rights. If subjective group rights are established as sacrosanct, then it is impossible to deny rights to any self-proclaimed group demanding such rights for itself. Freedom as a right is based on an individualist anthropology, which sees the individual, or even the group, as self-defined, free in its isolation and independence, yet in a constant state of antagonism or even fear that such freedom might be compromised by the demands of the other – a freedom which doesn't feel very free at all.

The American theologian Stanley Hauerwas shares these anxieties about rights language. Rights are fine when they simply express the social and legal duties we owe to one another, especially when adjudicating between strangers. However, they do not help when dealing with bonds between friends or neighbours, or between parents and children, for example. When the language of rights becomes our basic moral framework or instinct something has gone wrong. Rights can never be basic to the extent that kindness or generosity towards one another are. Healthy social life depends on a thick network of relations that holds people together through bonds of sympathy, compassion, patience and respect. When the language of rights becomes central, it diminishes the quality of the relationship, and tends to result in people shouting at each another across newspaper columns or on Twitter, each claiming their rights, rather than in healthy, fruitful and warm human bonds. Hauerwas quotes Simone Weil in this connection: 'to place the notion of rights at the centre of social conflicts is to inhibit any possible impulse of charity on both sides'.[12]

THE RECORD OF RIGHTS

The result of these difficulties is a disappointing record when it comes to actual delivery of human rights on the ground. Human rights legislation may be a valuable and worthwhile corrective to abuses of human dignity around

---

[12] Hauerwas, S. (2014), *The Work of Theology*. Grand Rapids, Eerdmans. See pp.191–207: 'How to Think Theologically about Rights'. The quotation from Simone Weil comes from Weil, S. (1962), *Selected Essays 1934–1943*. London, Oxford University Press, p.21.

the world, and the infringement of basic requirements of social life and respect, yet, despite almost universal belief and agreement on a set of human rights, the results are thin. If one of the systemic problems of the idea of human rights is its lack of specificity, and the subsequent difficulty of definition, this issues in what amounts to lip service paid, but little substantive difference made on the ground. Despite the almost universal recognition of human rights as a cardinal doctrine, so much that they have, in many people's eyes, replaced racism or communism as the over-arching meta-narrative of the twenty-first century, there does not seem to be any great advance in the observance of human rights in the world today. Around nine core human rights treaties have been ratified by most of the world's nations in continent after continent. Nonetheless, news of human rights abuses is depressingly common. China is often upbraided for its dismal human rights record; Brazil records a thousand killings by the police every year; across the Islamic world what in the West are usually considered the rights of women are commonly lacking, while Europe is showing signs of turning in nationalist directions again, with deep suspicion of its Muslim populations. Even the USA's continued use of drone strikes and torture in combat situations doesn't sit easily with human rights activism. Human trafficking, our modern form of slavery, abounds worldwide and shows little signs of disappearing, while children routinely work in mines and appalling conditions in factories across the globe. Human rights law has its value, yet the difficulty is that such treaties are not legally binding. They are aspirational. And aspirations don't necessarily translate into action, especially when economic, social or religious factors loom larger.

RIGHTS AND FREEDOM

Modern societies need a strong foundation for ensuring each person has access to some of the basic requirements for life: liberty, security, food, water, shelter, and so on. The question is whether 'rights' language is the best way to ensure it. In summary, there are perhaps two main problems such language faces.

The first goes back to the grounds on which rights are granted. Rights are based on the notion of equality – we can claim human rights only if we know what it is to be human. If it is almost impossible to identify some secret capacity which every human being possesses, some inner core that defines what it means to be human, then the notion threatens to become meaningless.

Ronald Dworkin argued that the notion of the equality of all human beings is so fundamental that it needs no justification.[13] However, when we step back and view the question historically and globally, the idea is far from self-evident. Hierarchical understandings of social life, whether in ancient Babylon, Chinese imperial history, the Roman Empire, early -modern Europe with its high value placed on respectability and noble birth, or modern Asian states with a caste system, have been much more common in human history. The notion of the equality of all human beings, their equal access to rights and freedom, needs some firm grounding rather than a vague assertion that it is true.

As we saw in chapter five, Larry Siedentop identified the early Christian movement as the birth of a sense of the individual as deserving of equal value, rather than the family

---

[13] Dworkin, R., (1992), 'In Defence of Equality', in R. J. Arneson (Ed.), *Liberalism*. Cheltenham: Edward Elgar, p.537.

or the tribe. The Christian idea of equality is rooted in the notion that every human being is made in the image of God – in other words, it is grounded in something external to them. Equality is based not on a capacity which every human being possesses, but on a designation given to them from the outside, as it were. Human beings are of equal worth because they are endowed with the divine image. They have a value given them from the outside. G.K. Chesterton used the image of coins. Humans, he claims, are as equal as pennies: they may look different, some are bright, some dull, some well used, some brand-new, but all are of equal value, not because of any quality held in the metal out of which they are made (which in itself is in fact worth very little), but because they bear the image of the sovereign, and are deemed to be worth something by the bearing of that image.[14]

Value grounded externally not internally, in being endowed with the image of God rather than possessing any particular internal capacity, is a much more solid and universal basis for human equality. In fact, it could be argued that, historically, a sense of egalitarianism has tended to arise in societies shaped by Christian faith. As Duncan Forrester argues: 'The ideal of equality haunts any culture that has been shaped or influence by Christianity'.[15]

The second difficulty refers to the question of who is to grant those rights. As Milbank and Hauerwas argue, if the state is to be the guarantor of human rights, that seems a

[14] I am indebted to Ramachandra, V. (2008), *Subverting Global Myths*. London, IVP, p.104 for this reference.
[15] Forrester, D. B. (2001), *On Human Worth: A Christian Vindication of Equality*. London, SCM, p.109.

ticket to a large, potentially oppressive state bureaucracy that in itself becomes a threat to personal and individual liberties and relationships; a dilemma lying at the heart of much recent political debate on both sides of the Atlantic. This then sets up an inevitably adversarial opposition between the one demanding their rights and everyone else (although it's hard to know who 'everyone else' really is) who are meant to deliver those rights. Unless we can answer with some conviction who is responsible for granting rights, then again the notion ends up meaning very little.

FREEDOM, GIFT AND LOVE

There is another way of viewing freedom, however: not so much as a right, but a gift. This idea has cropped up in several places on our journey. Augustine and Aquinas speak of freedom as a gift originally given, but forfeited in our exercise of it to turn away from God towards what is destructive and damaging. Paul and Luther speak of it as a gift subsequently re-given in Christ and received by faith. As we saw, for St Paul, the primary meaning of freedom is taken from his social setting. It is freedom from slavery into adoption as sons and daughters. Freedom is liberation from the powers that enslave, whether internal desires or external spiritual or material influences, into a new set of relationships. It is freedom, not from economic or social limitations on our liberty to act, but freedom from our own destructive desires or the powers that make us act in ways that will destroy us and all we hold dear. This is a different kind of freedom: not so much freedom to choose between good and evil, a freedom that has been lost, as a new freedom to actively choose the good. It is freedom for relationship, and a new sense of belonging.

Freedom from the destructive powers is granted as a gift from God, won by Christ and given as pure gift. John Barclay writes on this idea of grace as gift in St Paul.[16] In first-century Greco-Roman society, gifts were given to the deserving. They were a means of cementing social relations, and were most definitely given to deserving, worthy recipients. Paul was given grace, not because he was Jewish or morally upright, but simply because God chose to give him the gift. In the letter to the Galatians, Paul's Judaising opponents wanted to keep the new 'Christian' movement within the cultural boundaries of Judaism by insisting on circumcision, which for Paul was tantamount to 'nullifying the grace of God'. The gift of Christ is incongruous, given without reference to worth or ethnic identity. It cannot be understood by attempts to confine it within existing patterns of social or ethnic value. Grace was given to Paul not because he was either Jewish or virtuous. Gentiles were given grace, despite being Gentile. This vision required a new community which disregarded differences in social status, and so could experience freedom from social competitiveness, or the usual ethnic divisions in Greco-Roman society. This was an alternative vision to both the Roman honour culture and Jewish separateness.

In the letter to the Romans, Paul indicates that while the normal grammar of grace works on merit, God's grammar of grace works on a logic of 'despite' rather than 'because'. Abraham is chosen despite his lack of virtue or ethnic origin, not because of them. The nation of Israel was originally constituted by a gift of grace, unrelated to deserving, and is now, in Christ, opened up to Gentiles for inclusion. Gift therefore creates new kinds of people.

16 Barclay, J. M. G. (2015), *Paul and the Gift*. Grand Rapids, Eerdmans.

The gift of grace, given without regard to deserving, is a deeply subversive type of gift. A gift that is given because someone deserves it creates a relationship between equals, of those who merit grace. It fails to establish relationships between those who are not equals, and thus reinforces a stratified meritocracy. This theology of gift is directed towards the formation of new, innovative communities, where ethnic identities are not erased, but equally are not determinative, as is the case with all the other distinctions commonly dividing first-century Greco-Roman society, whether slave and free, male and female, Roman or barbarian. The social and cultural norms of society have been bypassed by the gift that creates a new community. The task Paul sets his readers is then to build such communities that learn to live that way.

The picture Barclay paints of Paul's vision of grace is that of a free gift, given without regard to deserts or social worth. It is therefore able to create relationship across differences of social standing, ethnicity or wealth. A community built on this kind of grace – grace as gift – learns to disregard differences of social status or ethnicity. It offers a freedom from the kind of competitive spirit we saw in the libertarian version of freedom, because it is not always trying to prove itself worthy of the gift. This theology of grace is directed towards the formation of new kinds of community, where ethnic and social differences are not entirely erased, but neither are they ultimately determinative.

When we use these ideas to apply to the notion of freedom, as opposed to grace, then we find something similar happening. Freedom for Paul is not a right but a gift. Freedom as a right asserted tends to create conflict, pitting the self against the other as a threat to my rights. It creates an economy of demand and delivery, a transactional relationship of the exchange of an object – whether freedom, education, water or healthcare – rather than the creation of a relationship. Furthermore, to deliver any actual results demands an ever more powerful state, seen as the guarantor of universal rights.

Freedom received as a gift creates a different kind of relationship with the one who gave the gift. This is one not based on deserving (which can of course fail once the recipient does something that fails to keep up the deserving), but on simple gratitude. Freedom as gift is directed not at independence from others, but interdependence with others. Modern secular ideas of freedom assert our freedom over others to choose our own way in life, our dress, our jobs, our lifestyle, free from the interference of others. It creates my own personal space of freedom of action, where I am alone in my own freedom. Freedom as gift turns a person out towards other recipients of the gift, in the sense that both St Paul and Luther saw – freedom as then dedicated to the service of others, not independence from them.

Moreover, freedom as gift sees the other not as a rival, or a threat to my freedom, but as a gift in him- or herself. Rather than another obstacle, there to threaten my liberty of action, they are instead an opportunity to express my freedom in this new set of relationships which Christian freedom brings. St Paul saw freedom as liberation from the 'powers' – forces that enslave and leave a person powerless before their own destructive desires which break human community and fellowship. It is the freedom of the adopted child, now a full member of society with a future; a new set of familial relationships, all based on the gift of grace. If we were to translate that into terms we might recognise, it would mean freedom from a whole set of social expectations that so often cramp and destroy lives. Freedom as the gift of God who gives value and worth means the teenager who realises she is free from the expectation to be thin, beautiful and confident before she can be acceptable and valued by her peers. It means freedom from the crippling loneliness felt by the elderly person in a modern city, with its individualistic and isolating mindset. It means the alcoholic who discovers the freedom not to take the extra drink. It means the banker who finds herself free from the need to acquire more and more money to prove her worth to her colleagues. It means the freedom of the refugee who, despite being treated as unwanted and unwelcome, knows that he is a child of God, endowed with dignity and rights based in that standing which no-one can take from him.

This vision goes beyond mere equality. A Christian vision of freedom as gift creates an economy of grace, a virtuous circle of grace and gratitude. It lays the emphasis on freedom used in the service of love. As St Paul put it: 'you were called to freedom, brothers and sisters; only do not use your freedom as an opportunity for self-indulgence, but through love become slaves to one another' (Gal. 5.13). Manumission, or freedom from slavery, created a sense of indebtedness to the one who gave the freedom. The freed slave was bound in a new relationship to the one who gave him freedom: a relationship no longer of slavery and compulsion, but of gratitude, more akin to the relationship of a child to a parent within the household, as Paul put it. A person who knows they have been given a precious gift is more likely, in turn, to become a giver as well as a recipient. The initial gift of freedom sets up a cycle of grace whereby, as both St Paul and Luther saw, we are set free to become voluntary servants of one another in love.

If I have been given freedom from enslavement to all kinds of powers that would otherwise limit my ability to thrive, then the logic of this freedom is gratitude to the one who gave the freedom. It means taking on responsibility to ensure, as far as I am able, that my neighbour has access to the same freedom. This then becomes a new way of thinking about rights. It is my responsibility to love my neighbour, in the basic terms of the Christian ethic of life: to ensure my neighbour has the basic means of life – liberty, security, food, water, shelter, education. The emphasis lies not so much on my right to those things, demanded from others, or from the state, but on my responsibility to ensure my neighbour has access to such things.

We considered earlier the question of who is meant to grant 'rights'. This vision, of freedom as not a right to be claimed, but a gift to be received, and then used in love and service to the neighbour, gives an answer: I am. I am responsible, as far as I am able, not to demand my own rights, but to ensure my neighbour has access to all that will enable her to thrive as God's creation, the potential recipient of grace. This is an economy of grace and gift that cannot be policed by a powerful state, but only motivated by a new way of thinking about rights and, at the end of the day, by a fresh breath of the Holy Spirit.

Vinoth Ramachandra, the Sri Lankan theologian, draws attention to a letter written by Bishop Azariah, the first Anglican bishop of India, along with 50 Dalit (and therefore low-caste) Christians in 1936, during the Indian movement for independence, when Christianity was criticised as a colonial oppressive religion:

Christianity has brought us fellowship and brother-hood. It has treated us with respect and it has given us self-respect. It has never despised us because of our lowly origin, but on the contrary has held us as individuals who are valuable before God and man as any man of any origin ... Best of all, Christianity has given us happiness and joy that can come only by the knowledge that the Lord has forgiven our sins and made us his children in Christ ... This has been the result of constant teaching, care and instruction. It has been accomplished, more-over, because we ourselves, freed by Christ from chains of ignorance and fear, have found within ourselves new courage, new hope, new strength to struggle upward.[17]

This is the voice of an authentic Christian vision of freedom.

The Christian vision of freedom offers something the libertarian or human rights visions do not. Those versions have their merits, establishing freedom from oppres-sion and asserting the right of individuals to certain basic elements essential to life. What they cannot do so well is to create community. What is needed is a vision of freedom that not only establishes freedom from oppression, but also a foundation for the kind of community life that stretches across the boundaries of ethnicity, class and the other divi-sions that separate people. This can only be found in the idea of freedom as gift and not right.

---

[17] Ramachandra, V. (2008), *Subverting Global Myths*. London, IVP, p.103.

10

Bound to Be Free

In this final chapter, it remains to draw together the threads of our discussion so far. We started with one of the great challenges facing global peace at present: the polarisation between a very liberalising view of human behaviour that sets a high value on autonomy, individual freedom, and personal choice, and other, often religious, worldviews which call for a much more controlled, disciplined and ordered approach to human life, and which see the liberalising tendencies of Western individualism as corrupt and decadent. We posed the question of whether there is another way of understanding freedom, one which avoids an atomising individualism that undermines any common sense of value and purpose, while also steering clear of the stifling and restrictive lack of liberty found in many societies around the world.

Our journey has taken us through wide stretches of intellectual history and to broad traditions of thinking on freedom. One simple but helpful structural approach to discussing freedom is the distinction used by Isaiah Berlin between 'freedom from' and 'freedom for'. This book has tried to mount a case for the broadly Pauline and

Augustinian tradition, as developed in such thinkers as Thomas Aquinas and Martin Luther, as a potential basis for our thinking on freedom that avoids some of the polarity we have mentioned. This final chapter will attempt to trace what this vision of freedom delivers us from, and what it delivers us for.

FREEDOM FROM ISOLATION

The libertarian vision of freedom assumes the autonomous individual as the basic unit of social life. John Locke envisages the free individual, liberated from innate pre-ordained ideas, or authorities past and present, as free to dispose of his property, time and possessions as he chooses, so long as he abides by the natural law that sets limits on his freedom. Jean-Jacques Rousseau sees the individual as liberated from the shackles of social custom and the assumed rules of society, free from the human interference of others who might lay all kinds of onerous expectations on this unique individual. Civilisation, and the communal life that goes with it, come off pretty badly in Rousseau's vision; freed from these shackles, the individual is able to return to a kind of state of nature, where freedom is found. John Stuart Mill is the great champion of free speech, and his philosophy is a charter for the individualist seeking to be free of a stifling social order which inhibits individuality and difference. John Milbank traces the roots of this radical emphasis on individual freedom much further back to William of Ockham and the Nominalist shift of the fourteenth century, a shift that saw the individual not as fundamentally oriented towards God and goodness, as Augustine and Aquinas had thought, but as radically free from any external influence whatsoever. This is the individual abstracted from any wider belonging to any universal concept of humanity: the 'punctual self', free in its own isolation.

With hindsight, we can perhaps see that these visions of the individual emerged in reaction to periods of history in Europe during which individual creativity was stifled. For the modern world, however, the legacy of this individualising tendency, and the understanding of freedom that went with it, is an increasing sense of individual isolation, and insulation within one's own personal space, with at the same time a desperate yearning to reach out and form real connection with others. This is relatively new. Social reforms in the UK (for example) in the nineteenth century, but above all the first half of the twentieth century – universal free education, unemployment insurance and pensions, a free national health service, public health programmes, the BBC, road and railway networks funded, like the welfare state, by taxation – all emerged out of a more social vision, one still animated by Christian notions of belonging and a directed freedom, a common vision of society in which we are properly dependent on one another. The transition towards the individualism seeded by the thinkers we have looked at in this book, and nurtured in the conditions of consumerist late modernity, sees these institutions now under threat.

The point has been made several times already that this newer vision of freedom identifies the other person as a threat, as an unwelcome boundary to an individual's own liberty of action and expression of desire. Even more, it threatens the dissolution of the individual altogether. As Terry Eagleton puts it:

> I am not truly free if I act out of my needs, interests and desires, since my liberty is then dependent on matters

which are external to it. To act as a woman, peace campaigner, or a Portuguese is to be less than unconstrained ... at its most perfected then, freedom would appear to vanish altogether ... Absolute freedom spells the death of difference.[1]

Absolute freedom which tries to eliminate restraint or limitation ends up destroying the individual itself, because without some kind of specificity, the self becomes a blank, an empty space lacking definition. Finiteness or limitation is not an evil, but is what it means to be a creature that is part of a wider creation – created to be in relation with, and in a sense defined by, relationship to other creatures, rather than in not-so-glorious isolation. What makes me 'me', is precisely what makes me different from you – that I am Christian, male, was born in Bristol, like cricket, dislike shopping, and so on. I am defined by specificity, by choices that have been made for me and choices I have made, not by the absolute potentiality of freedom. If everyone was like this, I would have no individuality, no distinctness as a person. I am defined by my relationship with others. Those boundaries that define the difference between me and others thus become not threats to my freedom, but the very thing that enables me to be free, to be who I am. As Richard Bauckham puts it: 'to deny our finitude is to refuse to be who we are, an impossible attempt to be something else'.[2]

We are created with limits placed upon us by our inability to thrive on our own, outside of a relationship with our

[1] Eagleton, T. (2005b), *Holy Terror*. Oxford, OUP, p.74.
[2] Bauckham, R. (2002), *God and the Crisis of Freedom: Biblical and Contemporary Perspectives*. Louisville, Westminster John Knox, p.39.

Creator or with our neighbour. Yet the libertarian vision sees those limits as an unfortunate restriction, so that, like the Platonic soul struggling to be free of the body, the modern self struggles to be free from the bonds that tie it to God and to other people.

It is not surprising that we face an epidemic of loneliness in modern life. Research suggests that in the UK, just over half of all people aged 75 and over live alone, and two-fifths of all older people (about 3.9 million) say the television is their main company. And the problem is not just with older people. A 2010 report from the Mental Health Foundation found that 18-to-34-year-olds were more likely to often feel lonely, to be anxious about feeling alone and to feel depressed because of loneliness, than the over-55s. There is an ongoing debate about the role of social media in the growth of loneliness, but it seems to play a complex role, as at the same time a symptom, a remedy and an exacerbation of the problem. The startling growth of social media demonstrates our deep desire to reach out and be connected. It provides means of connection beyond our personal space to others – particularly useful, for example, for elderly people at home alone – yet at the same time its competitive nature can make people feel more isolated, with other people's 'perfect lives' presented online in ways that feed envy and sometimes despair in those whose lives do not match up.

A good deal of scientific research suggests that loneliness is a major social disease in modern societies, can be twice as bad for people's health as obesity, and causes as many deaths worldwide as poverty. John Cacioppo suggests that chronic loneliness and its disastrous effects on human psychology question our normal assumption that the individual really is the basic unit of social life. He argues

that social co-operation is humanity's defining characteristic, and that to view ourselves primarily as individuals
in opposition to one another, in a Hobbesian, or even a
Lockean, sense is ultimately deeply damaging.[3] This leads
us to the surprising conclusion that, rather than freedom
meaning freedom from others to pursue our own ends, in
fact it may best be understood as freedom from ourselves.

We need freedom from isolation, loneliness, and being
left to our own devices. The kind of freedom trumpeted in
the libertarian view, when taken seriously and to its ultimate
conclusion, ends up ultimately being a kind of captivity:
each person locked in their own personal space, viewing
others with suspicion as competitors and a restraint on
the exercise of personal desire. What is needed is freedom
precisely from this isolating and restricting understanding
of human life and behaviour. Freedom is found, paradoxically, in the glad and welcome acceptance of the other as a
gift, not a threat; individuality which serves not to isolate us
from one another or from God, but which instead creates
relationship. It is found in a view of human life as essentially
communal before it is individual; that sees us constituted
first and foremost by our relationships, not our separateness.

FREEDOM FOR COMMUNITY

How can such a vision of life be sustained? The converse
of freedom from isolation is our need for freedom for
community. We need a vision of the self which is integrally
related to others; where freedom is found in our relationships, rather than apart from them. This is something the

---

[3] Cacioppo, J. T. & Patrick, W. (2008), *Loneliness: Human Nature and the Need for
Human Connection*. New York, Norton.

libertarian idea of freedom cannot deliver, because it always moves to relationship as a secondary move after the establishment of the individual as the basic unit of social life.

The Christian vision of freedom starts not with emancipation from God, but in relation with him. Human persons are constituted first and foremost by their existence as creatures created not to live in isolation, but to be related to God their Creator, and to one another: 'it is not good for a man to be alone' (Gen. 2.18). In other words, we are created for community, and only find true freedom in community.

Faced with the threat of Islamic terrorism, the secular idea of freedom espoused, for example, by the authors of *Charlie Hebdo* – the freedom to say or draw what they choose, regardless of whether it offends, the freedom asserted as a right over others, the freedom that sees the other not as a neighbour to be loved but an enemy to be resisted – is part of the problem, not part of the solution.

Our common understanding of the individual as the basic unit of society, the ultimate autonomous entity who has the right to determine his or her own future and destiny, is so much part of our mental furniture that it is sometimes a shock to realise how recent, and in some ways idiosyncratic, it is. For example, John Taylor, writing on African religion, gives an idea of a very different sense of the self from the one we are used to in the West:

Any attempt to look at the world through African eyes must involve this adventure of the imagination whereby we abandon our image of a man whose complex identity is encased within the shell of his physical being, and allow ourselves instead to visualize a centrifugal self-hood, equally complex, interpermeating other selves in a relationship in which subject and object are no longer distinguishable. 'I think therefore I am' is replaced by 'I participate therefore I am' ... To him, the individual is always an abstraction ... the underlying conviction remains that an individual who is cut off from the communal organism is a nothing.[4]

John Zizioulas, discussing Maximus the Confessor, writes: 'The substratum of existence is not Being but Love.'[5] The same insight is described by St Paul: 'if I do not have love I am nothing' (1 Cor.13.2) – and he meant it. What holds us in existence is not our own individual being, but the love which binds us to God and to others. We are not isolated dots, but knots in a net. Society is not a collection of individuals, but a network of relationships. Yet this can only be true if we emerged from Love itself, a God who is a perfect community of Love – the Trinitarian God of Christian faith. It is not so much that human society needs to be modelled on the Trinitarian life of God, the 'social Trinity' as developed by theologians such as Jürgen Moltmann and Leonardo Boff, but that human life is grounded in participation in the Trinitarian life of God. We don't need to try to imitate God, but to be in relationship to him.[6] It is when we try to break away from those roots into pure self-determination that the problems begin. We are, so Christian theology tells us, the creation of a God who is in his own life a community of three persons, perfectly united in will,

[4] Taylor, J. V. (1963), *The Primal Vision: Christian Presence amid African Religion.* London, SCM, pp.49–50, 93, 99.

[5] Zizioulas, J. D. (1985), *Being as Communion: Studies in Personhood and the Church.* London, Darton, Longman & Todd, p.97.

[6] The point is made powerfully by Fiddes, P. S. (2000), *Participating in God: a Pastoral Doctrine of the Trinity.* London, Darton Longman & Todd.

being and love. It makes sense that we are created precisely for and defined by our relationships of love.

It makes sense also to see how, for St Paul, freedom is the freedom to be our true selves, not in the sense that we can 'be whoever we want to be', but as we were created to be: liberated from our isolation and capable of giving ourselves in love and compassion to our neighbour: 'For you were called to freedom, brothers and sisters; only do not use your freedom as an opportunity for self-indulgence, but through love become slaves to one another' (Gal. 5.13). This is freedom not from being a slave but for being a full member of the family. It is not freedom into emptiness, freedom into nothingness, but freedom into a new set of relationships that fill that space, not in a limiting way, but in liberating us to enjoy our own created selves in relation with others.

As we saw earlier, Luther saw it in similar terms. The Christian's freedom is freedom to become the 'perfectly dutiful servant of all, subject to all'. The late medieval view of God, or even Christ as impartial judge, tended to encourage an idea of God that was a little like the neighbour in the libertarian view – a threat to our freedom. This often made him seem like a divine judge who was waiting to condemn, before whom the Christian needed to prove himself worthy of divine favour through good works. The good news of the gospel, for Luther, was that God is not first and foremost an impartial judge, but one who declares himself to be for us, on our side, as it were, in the gift of Christ, to be received by faith. This changes God from an enemy into a friend, from a threat into a source of grace and mercy. In faith, we find ourselves united with God in Christ in a closeness of union and communion.

Freed from the requirement to prove ourselves before God, or, for that matter, other people, seen as those from whom we need to somehow win approval, or prove ourselves worthy before, we become free for a new kind of relationship, based not on worth, or deserving, but on our belonging to Christ together in love. It is called the church.

In most human communities, relationships tend to be based on actual attraction, common interests, or like-minded thinking. We tend to club together with other like-minded people who share the same interests, background, class or ethnicity. From its beginning the Christian church was always meant to be a different kind of community, drawing people together not on the basis of similar tastes or backgrounds, but rather a vision of a new kind of humanity. Paul paints a picture of a community where there is 'no longer Greek and Jew, circumcised and uncircumcised, barbarian, Scythian, slave and free; but Christ is all and in all'. [7] In urban society during the Roman empire, ethnic and social division was rife. Riots between different ethnicities were common, and the ancient divisions between classes and religions were evident on every street corner. In that context, as Rodney Stark puts it,

> To cities filled with the homeless and impoverished, Christianity offered charity as well as hope. To cities filled with newcomers and strangers, Christianity offered an immediate basis for attachments. To cities filled with orphans and widows, Christianity offered a new and expanded sense of family. To cities torn by violent ethnic strife, Christianity offered a new basis for social solidarity. [8]

[7] Colossians 3.11.
[8] Stark, R. (1996), *The Rise of Christianity*. New York, HarperOne, p.161.

This was to be a community grounded not in identity found within oneself, whether of ethnic origin, racial profile, or class status, but in something outside oneself: a mutual recognition of common creaturely dependence on God, belonging to Jesus Christ, and a recognition of the same Holy Spirit of Christ present in each other.

People do not simply become Christians and then subsequently choose whether or not to join the church. It is the other way around. Becoming a Christian means, at its heart, joining the community of those who belong to Jesus Christ. It means becoming part of the church, sharing its life, becoming a part of the body, to use St Paul's memorable image. Paul points out how a hand does not exist on its own and then happen to choose to become part of the wider body – it only exists as part of that body, linked into the arm, and through that to every other part. To imagine it as separate from the body is to imagine it severed, lifeless and dead.[9] Christian identity is communal.

Because Christian faith sees human beings as created by a God who is a perfect community of love, it can sustain a view of the individual who finds her true identity, fulfilment and freedom in relation with others rather than on her own. It is, in David Kelsey's words, an 'Eccentric Existence', a life which is literally ex-centric, centred not within itself, but outside itself, in God.[10] We are in the fullest sense bound to be free – made to be free, but only finding true freedom precisely in our bonds with one another, not in isolation from one another. As Stanley Hauerwas puts it:

[9] 1 Corinthians 12.12–30.
[10] Kelsey, D. H. (2009), *Eccentric Existence: a Theological Anthropology*. Louisville, Ky., Westminster John Knox.

As Christians, we do not seek to be free but rather to be of use, for it is only by serving that we discover the freedom offered by God. We have learned that freedom cannot be had by becoming 'autonomous' – free from all claims except those we voluntarily accept – but rather freedom literally comes by having our self-absorption challenged by the needs of another.[11]

Christian freedom is not so much the freedom to choose, but the freedom to love. My neighbour is not a threat to or a limitation of my freedom but a gift to enable me to become more truly free. If the purpose of human life is, as Jesus Christ says, to become capable of love for God and my neighbour, then my neighbour in all his particularity, is in one sense offered to me as an opportunity to exercise love and compassion, the very thing I am here to learn, so that I can become more fully free, more fully human.

FREEDOM FROM SELF

The libertarian tradition sees freedom as freedom for self-determination, to express our natural desires, perhaps throwing off restraints to act according to one's true self. We have already seen one form of 'freedom from' – freedom from isolation – but there is another form of liberation needed, which, paradoxically, is freedom from ourselves.

In a perceptive and penetrating essay, Ellen Charry identifies the tendency to see emancipation from God as the route to freedom in the modern world.[12] Instead, she

[11] Hauerwas, S. (1999), *After Christendom? How the Church Is to Behave if Freedom, Justice, and a Christian Nation Are Bad Ideas*. Nashville, Abingdon Press, p.53.
[12] Charry, E., (1998), 'The Crisis of Modernity and the Christian Self', *A Passion for God's Reign*: 89-112. Grand Rapids: Eerdmans. There is further discussion of Charry's argument in Bauckham, R. (2002), *God and the Crisis of Freedom: Biblical and Contemporary Perspectives*. Louisville, Westminster John Knox, pp.188–197.

argues that emancipation from God is precisely the problem. The modern self is all about self-sufficiency, autonomy and freedom, and this absolute value of freedom leaves no opportunity for growth and development. Rousseau's notion was that a child needs freedom from restraint to grow into full maturity. Christian faith, as well as many other moral traditions down the ages, believes that training is necessary, and that training needs discipline and structure. In fact, it goes further, to say that to function well as human beings, we need not so much emancipation, but God. The child needs to grow up. And the child needs guidance and direction from a parent to know what or who to grow up into. The lack of any wider framework into which one might grow into maturity, a direction towards which growth might happen – for example, rethinking ourselves as modelled on God's Trinitarian life, through recognition that my own self is the image of God, as St Augustine saw it – leaves the self without any moral or social infrastructure. As a result of clinging to freedom as an absolute value, modern Western societies, Charry suggests, neglect the formation of their citizens. Christian faith, on the other hand, gives not so much freedom from society as freedom from the pressure of society to conform to debased ideas of what it means to be human – in other words, to be famous, rich, slim, tanned, and so on.

We need freedom from the untutored self, the immature self that is liable to chase after desires that are dead ends, childish longings which attach themselves to trivia rather than what is of lasting value. Rather than needing freedom for the self, we need freedom from the self. Even more than this, we need freedom from the habits that tend to destroy lives, communities, marriages, families and even the planet on which we live.

Rousseau assumed that the self, freed from the constraints of a corrupting civilisation, will be able to rebuild a higher civilisation based on the purity of its original state of nature. John Locke, with his idea that the mind is a blank slate, upon which experience writes our ideas and knowledge of the world, effectively eliminated the idea of original sin. The Augustinian, Thomist and Reformation view of the self did not see the mind as a *tabula rasa*, but rather as a blotted sheet, already stained and twisted by the habits of sin inherited from previous generations. The idea of original sin is, in fact, a corollary of the very communal view of humanity outlined above. If we are essentially constituted by our relationships with God and each other, and at some early stage of human evolution some fundamental fracture in those relationships took place, then that could never just affect the one who caused the break, but would ripple out into the whole of humanity, so that, in Augustine's famous image, the human race becomes a corporate *massa peccati*.

If this is in any way true, what is required for freedom is not so much the removal of restraint, leaving the self free to create itself in its own image, but the overcoming of deeply ingrained habits of self-centredness which destroy the very relationships that bring fulfilment and freedom. The libertarian vision, centred as it is on the individual self, is exactly the problem. It views the world as a canvas for self-projection, seeing the self as free to pursue its own whims and desires, when so often it is those very whims and desires that prove destructive. Christian faith has developed a taxonomy of sin, which can at times feel like a worrying preoccupation with evil, a morbid fascination with the lurid details of lasciviousness, yet at its best is a way of helping people overcome the very habits that, once ingrained in the psyche, slowly unravel social bonds and all that makes life worth living.

The idea of the 'Seven Deadly Sins', of Pride, Envy, Gluttony, Lust, Anger, Greed and Sloth, emerged as a neat way of remembering some of the chief ways in which this deadly pattern of behaviour manifested itself. The origins of the list are obscure. One possibility is that they came from a list of eight bad habits drawn up by Evagrius of Pontus, the fourth-century Greek monastic theologian. Around 200 years later, while writing a book of reflections on the book of Job, Pope Gregory the Great reduced the list to seven, and the number stuck. The list has shifted over time, with the exact items included and the order in which they came varying from one list to another, but it caught the imagination as a tool to understand the moral life, or better, the immoral life. By the time of the high Middle Ages, it had become a standard way of organising sin – a useful taxonomy of misbehaviour. Perhaps the most famous treatment of all came in Dante's *Divine Comedy*, where he described his own dream-expedition through hell, purgatory and heaven as a journey of exploration, purging and redemption of these seven fatal habits. Thomas Aquinas gave a classic analysis of the seven sins in his *De Malo*, On Evil, written in the 1270s, and used the list extensively in his great *Summa Theologiae*. It continues to serve as a picture of the debased, diseased self from which we need deliverance.[13]

St Paul's characteristic description of Christian liberation, therefore, is freedom from oppression and freedom from this intricate and convoluted pattern of sin.[14] It is freedom

---

[13] See Tomlin, G. (2014), *The Seven Deadly Sins; How to Overcome Life's Most Toxic Habits*. Oxford, Lion Hudson, for a discussion and exploration of this.
[14] For example, Romans 6.7, 18; 6.22; 8.2.

that results from God's dramatic intervention into human history in Jesus Christ, breaking the power of habits that enslave, and elicits, in the first instance, a simple belief in the freedom that has resulted from that intervention. We do not need to obey the 'powers', whether of sin and death, or the needs created by advertising and marketing, or the oppressive political or economic forces that dominate and suppress human flourishing.[15] This liberation then leads to freedom from the very patterns of behaviour that destroy. We are particularly aware of this today in our knowledge that the planet on which we live cannot long survive our unlimited consumption, our satisfaction of our own desire for energy, space and plastic, which is slowly clogging up our seas, opening holes in the ozone layer and melting polar ice caps. There is a profound structure to the natural world: a rhythm of life and order we urgently need to observe and respect. The dream of unfettered freedom might have seemed feasible in the period of the early Enlightenment, when it coincided with the Industrial Revolution, which promised unparalleled power over nature, and the freedom to do as we wished with it, but now we are more chastened – humbled, even. Unless we learn the self-discipline to control the exercise of our freedom to consume the resources of the earth, respecting the order that inheres in the natural world, our very survival is imperilled, let alone the future of the planet itself.

We used to think that freedom to live well on this planet meant control over nature, and liberation from the ties of

---

[15] This of course is a theme developed in the various kinds of liberation theology that have developed in the twentieth century. These approaches have helpfully analysed the forms of social and political oppression which inhibit human flourishing, yet they sometimes need a stronger sense of the church as the alternative community outlined in the previous section, as well as a clearer shape of the form of Christian freedom into which social and political liberation delivers us.

place and space that we examined in chapter one. Now we are perhaps learning to think differently. Freedom requires not emancipation from nature, but an ideology that both binds us to nature and makes us conscious of a responsibility for it. The Christian doctrine of creation does just this. It tells us that we are part of the natural world, bound to it, made out of the same stuff as everything else. In one sense, we are just highly developed animals, with physical bodies vulnerable to decay like any other form of life. At the same time, it tells us that we are given a particular role within creation, to bear the image of God and care for the creation in God's name. The part of the creation story found in Genesis 2, which says that 'the Lord God formed man from the dust of the ground, and breathed into his nostrils the breath of life', emphasises the first of these two insights, while the first part of the story in Genesis 1, where we are told that 'God created humankind in his image, in the image of God he created them', emphasises the latter.

Freedom to live wisely and well within our proper creaturely limitations means freedom from our selves – those selves that simply want what serves our own interests, what satisfies us. Such habits are so deeply entrenched in us that a serious process of purging, of relearning new habits, is required – in short, a very different understanding of freedom.

FREEDOM FOR GOD

In chapter four, we explored Iris Murdoch's and Simone Weil's doubts about a directionless form of freedom, and their sense of a need for a freedom that lies close to a form of obedience, an orientation to the good, or to God. Going further, the debate we traced in chapter seven, between

Aquinas on the one hand and Ockham and Scotus on the other, centred on the nature of human freedom. Was it at the end of the day a kind of 'freedom of indifference', where people are free to choose out of any number of options without any external influence at all? Or is it a 'freedom for excellence', where we have an inbuilt, created orientation towards God, goodness and truth?

In chapter eight we saw Luther's opposition, despite his Nominalistic training as a young theologian, to the Ockhamist view of the self and its freedom. The idea of the free self, uninfluenced by any external attraction, is a fiction. The human soul is a beast of burden ridden either by God or the devil, pulled one way or another. Expressed in less dramatic language, we are always captivated by something outside ourselves, and drawn to the object of our desire, whatever that may be. On this point, Luther agrees with Aquinas – we are made for God, even if that underlying longing has become disorientated by sin, like a homing device that has been interfered with and gets diverted onto a lesser target.

Remember the image of the child learning to play the piano, and thus becoming free to play the tunes she loves? Or the man who dedicates himself to learning a language so he is free to converse in it to anyone he meets in his expatriate life? This is a kind of freedom that has to be learnt, by a slow, steady dedication to a regime of discipline that gradually shapes the soul into freedom. It is freedom to be what we were always meant to be: the freedom to be our true created selves.

We often hear the language of being 'true to myself', or 'finding myself', as a plea for authenticity and the pathway to personal fulfilment. The basic idea, fed by those eighteenth-century convictions that the true self in a state of nature is pure and unsullied, is that if we were able to peel off every layer of expectation laid upon us by society, the artificial constructions of identity, gender, class, and occupation, we would find our true selves hidden within, like a cook preparing an artichoke, peeling away the rough leaves to find the tender heart within. Yet what if we are in fact more like onions than artichokes? What if, when we peel away the expectations of others, the roles we play in society in relation to others, there is nothing there? What if there is no mysterious self waiting to be discovered, no essence of 'me' that is stifled by the irritating other people who expect me to play roles prescribed for me? The common assumption is that we have 'selves' waiting to be found, yet, as Charles Taylor argues in his magisterial work on the Modern Self, the idea that we have 'selves, the way we have heads or arms, and inner depths, the way we have hearts or livers, as a matter of hard interpretation-free fact' is a relatively modern notion, one rooted in our late modern, Western view of the world.[16]

An alternative, and much more ancient, view is that our selves are not so much discovered as created. We create our inner selves over our lifetimes by the commitments we make, the relationships we form, the habits we let take root, the way we react to what happens to us. In a sense, a new-born baby has a self, but it is a malleable self, waiting to be formed, shaped and moulded. In Christian terms, it does not start with a complete blank slate, as Locke thought it did, because it is bound in to the human race, the family

---

[16] Taylor, C. (1989), *Sources of the Self: The Making of the Modern Identity*. Cambridge, CUP, pp.111–112.

and community into which it was born, affected by decisions made even before it was born – tangibly so when it comes to drug use, or illness in a mother which transfers to a child in the womb, or in the more subtle, hidden ways that begin to affect the child from early days. Yet, as the child grows, he is shaped by what happens to him: broken bones, joyful or painful experiences of family life, where parents choose to live, or decisions he makes of what friends to choose, what loyalties to adopt, who to marry, what job to do.

Our selves are created by what happens to us and the decisions we make, in relation to other people. And so we develop our selves, in relation to parents, siblings, friends, teachers, colleagues, neighbours. And our likeness to and difference from these people constitutes our own sense of self. We are defined by our relationships and our commitments, not by our self-directed freedom.

James Rebanks's book *The Shepherd's Life* is a remarkable tale of a man who has found happiness, not in the delights of urban life but in a freely chosen return to his forefathers' practices of being a shepherd in the English Lake District. The book describes his journey through a degree at Oxford University, the lures of a life in the city, and the decision to return to his roots to learn the ancient practices of sheep farming. Turning his back on the 'freedoms' of urban life, he chooses a difficult path: early mornings, harsh weather, disappointments with lost and dying sheep. It is a way of life that slowly builds up skill, expertise and wisdom. It closes off all kinds of other options that many of us would find hard to resist, yet the last line of the book reads, 'This is my life. I want no other'. Here is a happy man, one who is defined by the commitments he has made, to his community and to his trade. Happiness is not found in unbridled freedom, but precisely in the commitments and choices we make.[17]

Now, this process can be random, shaped by what happens to us and instinctive decisions made by us. Or it can be deliberately shaped towards a goal. The theology we saw developed in Thomas Aquinas suggested that our natural orientation is towards God and goodness, so that true freedom, the freedom to be our true selves, is found in orienting ourselves towards the One who gave us life, the One who created us, and the people we find alongside us, who are given to us as an object of respect and love – or, in the words of Jesus, in loving God and neighbour.

Unfortunately, this no longer happens as a matter of course. An Augustinian and Thomist anthropology would suggest that without the fall, human beings would naturally grow towards God and goodness as a plant naturally grows towards the sun. In our current fallen state, however, we are drawn in all kinds of directions, mistaking other objects for the true object of beauty and truth, just as a malfunctioning satnav leads an unsuspecting driver in entirely the wrong direction.

Freedom is not something we can simply assume; it is a gift we have to learn how to use. It is like someone being given a sailing boat as a present, who then has to learn how to sail, otherwise the boat will either languish unused, get damaged, or even sink, taking down boat and sailor with it.

St Paul talks in these terms when he discusses the new dispensation, the ministry of the Spirit: 'Now the Lord is the Spirit, and where the Spirit of the Lord is, there is freedom. And all of us, with unveiled faces, seeing the glory of

---

[17] Rebanks, J. (2016), *The Shepherd's Life: A Tale of the Lake District*. London, Penguin.

the Lord as though reflected in a mirror, are being transformed into the same image from one degree of glory to another; for this comes from the Lord, the Spirit' (2 Cor. 3.17–18). The Holy Spirit brings a new freedom to the Christian who is in relationship with God. Yet this freedom is not the liberty to fix our gaze on whatever we like, regardless of its value or beauty: it is precisely the freedom to see and focus our gaze on 'the glory of the Lord', the object of ultimate beauty, truth and goodness. It is freedom for God. The metaphor is of looking intently at something, so that the observer comes to resemble the object of attention, just as a mirror reflects the one who is looking at it. The Spirit arrests our attention so we watch the gripping match, not the clouds drifting by. By exercising this freedom, the ability to see and be transfixed by the object of true goodness and beauty, the Christian comes to resemble Christ, the image of God. This image was given at creation, and yet needs to be restored and refreshed, bringing with it the ability to love the other; to rejoice in goodness; to overcome self-centredness and isolation; to live a full human life, which actually ends up looking like divine life – the life of Jesus Christ the One, in whom divinity and humanity are joined.

This habit of attention, however, needs training, just as did the desire to play Mozart's piano concertos, or learn German. The right use of freedom, the freedom for excellence, is learnt through steady habits of discipline to a particular object. In the Christian tradition of spiritual life that means the exercise of the traditional disciplines of engagement (study, worship, service, prayer, fellowship, confession, etc.), as well as the disciplines of abstinence (such as solitude, silence, fasting, frugality, sacrifice). These disciplines were always seen as a kind of spiritual coaching, training the heart and soul to focus attention on what matters, and not to get sidelined onto trivia such as wealth, sex, fame or power.[18] They were like the tennis player's regular, repeated and sometimes monotonous practice that trains the body to play the right shot instinctively when the time comes to play it in a match. In the same way, these disciplines enabled the mind, soul and body to focus attention on God, rather than get distracted onto other things.

Freedom for God turns out not to be the stifling, heteronomous submission to laws, rules and expectations that hem us in and restrict us. Instead it becomes freedom to be what we were created to be. It is the freedom of the person who has voluntarily submitted to a regime of physical exercise and good diet, who is now able to use the bodily fitness acquired to play tennis, run up stairs, feel healthy and live a life free of physical pain and discomfort.[19]

Rather than trying to free ourselves from God to determine our own identities and selves, the path to true freedom begins and ends in relationship. It begins in cultivating relationship with the God who is self-giving, mutually enriching love in his very being. This involves being grafted into relationship with an entirely new kind of community: one drawn together, not by mutual interest or attraction, but by baptism – a deep immersion into the life of God in Christ through the Holy Spirit, and those others who belong to him. In this fellowship, through constant reminders of the goodness of God and the calling of human life, and through

[18] See Tomlin, G. (2006), *Spiritual Fitness: Christian Character in a Consumer Culture.* London, Continuum for a discussion of the traditional disciplines as training in holiness.
[19] Ibid., chapter 3.

regular disciplines that train the mind, soul and heart, we find freedom from isolation, and from the self-centredness that imprisons us in our own self-protected space. And we learn the freedom for community and freedom for God – the freedom to love, which is the greatest freedom of all.

If the West is to respond to some of the greatest challenges it faces today, whether the challenge of a destructive, militant Islamism, or the tendency to divide into nationalistic isolation, or a refugee crisis that threatens to disturb the equilibrium of our societies, it will need more intellectual and moral resources than are offered by the libertarian tradition. It does need a vision of freedom, but it must be more focused and disciplined than anything that tradition can bring. The Christian tradition offers such a vision from its rich history of thought and moral formation. Today, more than ever, we need the freedom of the saints who learnt how to use the gift of freedom for what really matters.

Jesus taught that the secret of living well is to learn to love God and love your neighbour, not to find ways to be liberated from them. The paradox of freedom is that it is not in being free from God and neighbour that we find true liberty, but that we find it growing through welcoming and strengthening the very ties that bind us to our Creator and those he gives us to love.

BIBLIOGRAPHY

Anselm, 'On Freedom of Choice', in ed. Williams, T. (2007), *Anselm: Basic Writings*. Indianapolis: Hackett.

Aquinas, T. (2003), *On Evil*. Oxford: Oxford University Press.

Augustine, ed. Burleigh, J.H.S. (1953), *On Free Will*. London: SCM.

Augustine (1991), *Against Two Letters of the Pelagians*. Edinburgh: T. & T. Clark.

Augustine, 'On Nature and Grace', in ed. Schaff, P. (1991), *St Augustine: Writings Against the Pelagia*ns. Edinburgh: T. & T. Clark.

Augustine (1998), *Confessions*. Oxford: Oxford University Press.

Augustine (1998), *The City of God against the Pagans*. Cambridge: Cambridge University Press.

Barber, B.R. (1996), *Jihad vs. McWorld*. New York: Ballantine.

Barclay, J.M.G. (2015), *Paul and the Gift*. Grand Rapids: Eerdmans.

Bauckham, R. (2002), *God and the Crisis of Freedom: Biblical and Contemporary Perspectives*. Louisville; Westminster: John Knox.

Bauman, Z. (1988), *Freedom*. Milton Keynes: Open University Press.

Bauman, Z. (1998), *Globalization: The Human Consequences*. Cambridge: Polity.

Berlin, I. (2002), 'John Stuart Mill and the Ends of Life' and 'Two Concepts of Liberty' in *Liberty*. Oxford: Oxford University Press.

Boehner, P., ed. (1990), *Ockham: Philosophical Writings*. Indianapolis: Hackett.

Bonner, G. (2006), *Freedom and Necessity: St. Augustine's Teaching on Divine Power and Human Freedom*. Washington, DC: Catholic University of America Press.

Booth, K.D., ed. (2002), *Worlds in Collision: Terror and the Future of Global Order*. Basingstoke: Palgrave Macmillan.

Bornkamm, H. (1983), *Luther in Mid-Career*. London: Darton, Longman and Todd.

Cacioppo, J.T. and Patrick, W. (2008), *Loneliness: Human Nature and the Need for Human Connection*. New York: W.W. Norton.

Campbell, D. (2009), *The Deliverance of God: An Apocalyptic Re-Reading of Justification in Paul*. Grand Rapids: Eerdmans.

Chadwick, H. (2009), *Augustine of Hippo: A Life*. Oxford: Oxford University Press.

Charry, E. (1998), 'The Crisis of Modernity and the Christian Self' in *A Passion for God's Reign*. Grand Rapids: Eerdmans.

Chesterton, G.K. (1986), *Saint Thomas Aquinas, Saint Francis of Assisi*. San Francisco: Ignatius Press.

Conradi, P. (2001), *Iris Murdoch: A Life*. New York: W.W. Norton.

Dworkin, R., 'In Defence of Equality' in Arneson, R.J. (1992), *Liberalism*. Cheltenham: Edward Elgar.

Eagleton, T. (2005), *Holy Terror*. Oxford: Oxford University Press.

Eagleton, T. (2014), *Culture and the Death of God*. New Haven: Yale University Press.

Ebeling, G. (1972), *Luther: An Introduction to His Thought*. London: William Collins.

Evans, G.R. (1982), *Augustine on Evil*. Cambridge: Cambridge University Press.

Fiddes, P.S. (2000), *Participating in God: A Pastoral Doctrine of the Trinity*. London: Darton, Longman and Todd.

Forde, G.O. (2005), *The Captivation of the Will: Luther vs. Erasmus on Freedom and Bondage*. Grand Rapids: Eerdmans.

Forrester, D. B. (2001), *On Human Worth: A Christian Vindication of Equality*. London: SCM.

Friedman, M. (1962), *Capitalism and Freedom*. Chicago: University of Chicago Press.

Friedman, M. and Friedman R. D. (1980), *Free to Choose: A Personal Statement*. New York, London: Harcourt, Brace Jovanovich.

Fromm, E. (2001), *The Fear of Freedom*. London: Routledge.

Fukuyama, F. (1992), *The End of History and the Last Man*. London: Penguin.

Fung, R.Y.K. (1988), *The Epistle to the Galatians*. Grand Rapids: Eerdmans.

Gaine, S. (2003), *Will There Be Free Will in Heaven?: Freedom, Impeccability and Beatitude*. London: Continuum.

Gay, P. (1969), *The Enlightenment: The Science of Freedom*. New York: W.W. Norton.

Gerrish, B.A. (1982), *The Old Protestantism and the New: Essays on the Reformation Heritage*. Edinburgh: T. & T. Clark.

Gibb, H.A.R. (1953), *Islam*. Oxford: Oxford University Press.

Giddens, A. (2002), *Runaway World: How Globalisation is Reshaping Our Lives*. London: Profile Books.

Gray, J. (1995), *Enlightenment's Wake: Politics and Culture at the Close of the Modern Age*. London: Routledge.

Gray, J. (2004), *Heresies Against Progress and Other Illusions*. London: Granta.

Gray, J. (2015), *The Soul of the Marionette: A Short Enquiry into Human Freedom*. London: Allen Lane.

Hauerwas, S. (1999), *After Christendom? How the Church Is to Behave if Freedom, Justice, and a Christian Nation Are Bad Ideas*. Nashville: Abingdon Press.

Hauerwas, S. (2014), *The Work of Theology*. Grand Rapids: Eerdmans.

Hinlicky, P.R. (2010), *Luther and the Beloved Community: A Path for Christian Theology After Christendom*. Grand Rapids: Eerdmans.

Hollingworth, M. (2013), *Saint Augustine of Hippo: An Intellectual Biography*. London: Bloomsbury.

Hunt, L. (2007), *Inventing Human Rights: A History*. New York: W.W. Norton.

Huntingdon, S.P. (2002), *The Clash of Civilisations and the Remaking of World Order*. London: Simon & Schuster.

Iserloh, E. (1968), *The Theses Were Not Posted*. London: Geoffrey Chapman.

Jenson, R. (1994), 'An Ontology of Freedom in the *De Servo Arbitrio* of Luther' in *Modern Theology* 10(3), 247–252.

Kelsey, D.H. (2009), *Eccentric Existence: A Theological Anthropology*. Louisville: Westminster John Knox.

Locke, J., ed. Laslett, P. (2015), *Two Treatises on Government*. Cambridge: Cambridge University Press.

Luther, M. (1960–90), *Luther's Works*. Philadelphia: Fortress Press.

Martyn, J. L. (1997), *Galatians*. New Haven: Yale University Press.

McCullough, L. (2014), *The Religious Philosophy of Simone Weil*. London: I.B. Tauris.

McGrath, A. E. (1987), *The Intellectual Origins of the European Reformation*. Oxford: Blackwell.

Milbank, J. (1990), *Theology and Social Theory: Beyond Secular Reason*. Oxford: Blackwell.

Milbank, J. (2009), 'Against Human Rights'. Retrieved 13 February 2017 http://www.theologyphilosophycenter.co.uk/papers/ Milbank_AgainstHumanRights.pdf.

Mill, J.S. (1998), *On Liberty and Other Essays*. Oxford: Oxford University Press.

Moyn, S. (2010), *The Last Utopia: Human Rights in History*. Cambridge, MA: Belknap.

Moyn, S. (2014), *Human Rights and the Uses of History*. London: Verso.

Murdoch, I. (1971), *The Sovereignty of Good*. London: Routledge.

Murdoch, I. (2003), *Metaphysics as a Guide to Morals*. London: Vintage.

Oberman, H.A. (1963), *The Harvest of Medieval Theology: Gabriel Biel and Late Medieval Nominalism*. Cambridge, MA: Harvard University Press.

O'Brien, R. (1992), *Global Financial Integration: The End of Geography*. London: Chatham House/Pinter.

O'Connor, Flannery, ed. Ellsberg, R. and Giannone, R. (2003), *Flannery O'Connor: Spiritual Writings*, Modern Spiritual Masters Series. New York: Orbis.

Pinker, S. (1998), *How the Mind Works*. London: Penguin.

Posner, E. (2014), *The Twilight of Human Rights Law*. Oxford: Oxford University Press.

Rajchman, J. (1985), *Michel Foucault: The Freedom of Philosophy*. Guildford, NY: Columbia University Press.

Ramachandra, V. (2008), *Subverting Global Myths*. London: IVP.

Rousseau, J.-J. (1987), 'The Social Contract' in *The Basic Political Writings*. Indianapolis: Hackett.

Rousseau, J.-J. (1991), *Émile or On Education*. London: Penguin.

Ruthven, M. (2002), *A Fury for God: The Islamist Attack on America*. London: Granta.

Schwartz, B. (2004), *The Paradox of Choice: Why More Is Less*. New York: HarperCollins.

Sheridan, A. (1980), *Michel Foucault: The Will to Truth*. London: Routledge.

Siedentop, L. (2014), *Inventing the Individual: The Origins of Western Liberalism*. London: Allen Lane.

Smith, J.K.A. (2009), *Desiring the Kingdom: Worship, Worldview and Cultural Formation*. Grand Rapids: Baker Academic.

Stark, R. (1996), *The Rise of Christianity*. New York: HarperOne.

Strawson, G. (2010), *Freedom and Belief*. New York: Oxford University Press.

Taylor, C. (1989), *Sources of the Self: The Making of the Modern Identity*. Cambridge: Cambridge University Press.

Taylor, C. (1991), *The Ethics of Authenticity*. Cambridge, MA and London: Harvard University Press.

Taylor, C. (2011), 'Conditions of an Unforced Consensus on Human Rights' in *Dilemmas and Connections*. Cambridge, MA: Harvard University Press.

Taylor, J.V. (1963), *The Primal Vision: Christian Presence amid African Religion*. London: SCM.

Thiselton, A.C. (1995), *Interpreting God and the Postmodern Self: On Meaning, Manipulation and Promise*. Edinburgh: T. & T. Clark.

Tilling, C., 'Paul, Evil and Justification Debates' in ed. Keith, C. and Stuckenbruck, L.T. (2016), *Evil in Second Temple Judaism and Early Christianity*. Tübingen: Mohr Siebeck.

Tilling, C., ed. (2014), *Beyond Old and New Perspectives on Paul: Reflections on the Work of Douglas Campbell*. Eugene: Cascade.

Toffler, A. (1970), *Future Shock*. London: Pan.

Tomlin, G. (2006), *Spiritual Fitness: Christian Character in a Consumer Culture*. London: Continuum.

Tomlin, G. (2011), *The Prodigal Spirit: The Trinity, the Church and the Future of the World*. London: Alpha International.

Tomlin, G. (2014), *The Seven Deadly Sins: How to Overcome Life's Most Toxic Habits*. Oxford: Lion Hudson.

Tomlin, G. (2017), *Luther's Gospel: Reimagining the World*. London: Bloomsbury.

Weil, S. (1952), *The Need for Roots*. Abingdon: Routledge.

Weil, S. (1962), *Selected Essays 1934–1943*. London: Oxford University Press.

Weil, S. (2009), *Waiting for God*. New York: Harper Perennial.

Zizioulas, J.D. (1985), *Being as Communion: Studies in Personhood and the Church*. London: Darton, Longman and Todd.

INDEX

A NOTE ON THE AUTHOR

Graham Tomlin is the Bishop of Kensington and the President of St Mellitus College. He taught Theology at Oxford University for several years, and is the author of many books, including *Looking Through the* Cross: *the Archbishop of Canterbury's Lent Book 2014,* and most recently *The Widening Circle: Priesthood as God's Way of Blessing the World.*

A NOTE ON THE TYPE

The text of this book is set in Minion, a digital typeface designed by Robert Slimbach in 1990 for Adobe Systems. The name comes from the traditional naming system for type sizes, in which minion is between nonpareil and brevier. It is inspired by late Renaissance-era type.